ADULT EDUCATION AND WORLDVIEW CONSTRUCTION

Adult Education and Worldview Construction

Leon McKenzie, Ed. D.

KRIEGER PUBLISHING COMPANY
MALABAR, FLORIDA
1991

Original Edition 1991

Printed and Published by
KRIEGER PUBLISHING COMPANY
KRIEGER DRIVE
MALABAR, FLORIDA 32950

Library of Congress Cataloging-in-Publication Data
McKenzie, Leon.
   Adult education and worldview contruction / by Leon McKenzie.
      p.   cm.
   ISBN 0-89464-488-2
   1. Adult education. 2. Adult education—Philosophy. I. Title.
LC5215.M35 1990
374—dc20   90-38004
                                                      CIP

10   9   8   7   6   5   4   3   2

Contents

Foreword

A consensus has been formed among adult education theorists that educational processes should serve purposes beyond the accomplishment of stated program objectives and the mastery of specific skills and knowledge. At the conclusion of any adult education program the participants should have somehow become more authentic human beings, more sensitive to the world in which they live, more eager to contribute to the civilizing process, and more able to identify options and opportunities available to them in the workaday world. Adult education theorists express these transcendent educational goals in a variety of ways. I believe it is fruitful to frame the higher purposes of adult education in terms of worldview construction for two reasons.

First, worldview construction is a comprehensive concept within which the discrete but similar aims of adult education, as expressed by a number of theorists, are brought together. This is shown in Chapter Seven. Second, worldview construction involves the ongoing development and maturation of understanding: understanding of the world, of others, of self, of understanding itself. Understanding is fundamental to being human. When sensual appetites have faded, when the hunger for wealth, power, and fame has been satisfied, there remains for us the profound need to understand. Someone once noted when we are born we arrive, as it were, in the middle of a conversation; we feel compelled to participate in the conversation and to contribute to it. Lacking some kind of understanding we cannot participate, we cannot contribute our small insights to the fund of insights that has been building for thousands of years.

Worldview construction, as a transcendent aim of adult education, can be facilitated tacitly or explicitly within the framework of any educational activity. That is, there is a potential for facilitating worldview construction in a variety of adult education contexts. Alternatively, worldview construction can itself become the direct focus of learning experiences in groups. The linkage of the concepts of worldview construction and adult education, it is hoped, will also open new areas of theoretical reflection among adult educators. This is to say that there is a way of helping adults change without assuming that their minds need to be invaded by a superior teacher or that they need to be emancipated or redeemed from false consciousness.

What at first seemed a simple juxtaposition of concepts—worldview construction and adult education—took on many dimensions as I initiated research, reflected on worldview construction, and began to set my thoughts to paper. Some of the issues involved in worldview construction are highly complex. I felt challenged at every turn to maintain a "sense of audience" and to express myself with as great a clarity as I could manage. Because of the complexity involved in relating worldview construction to adult education, I determined to offer here an overview of the ideas presented in the following pages. The purpose of this overview is to enable the reader to view the themes of each chapter within a framework that facilitates understanding.

Chapter One responds to the question "What is a worldview?" Building on the work of Martin Heidegger I define worldview in two ways. First, a worldview is a vantage point in time and culture that conditions a person's experience of the world. Second, a worldview is described as a person's understanding of the world. Understanding is in a continuing state of construction. This interpretive understanding comes about as a result of the individual's reflection on experience. Worldview construction is a naturally occurring process for all normally functioning adults. A worldview is not necessarily synonomous with a formal, systematic philosophy of life.

A singular problem comes to the fore in Chapter One because of my reliance on the work of the late Martin Heidegger. I recognize that many adult educators in North America are not familiar with Heidegger's phenomenology. More to the point, translations of some of his German neologisms sometimes seem awkward and unusual. For example, his use of the word *Dasein* to designate the being of being human appears strange until one realizes he attempted to show strikingly that the being of being human is utterly distinctive and separate from the being of inanimate material. For most of the history of philosophy the concept of being, the Latin *ens,* encompassed all reality without discriminating human from non-human reality. Again, Heidegger's use of the notion *In-der-Welt-sein,* being-in-the-world, seems unwieldy. He meant several things by this expression but the foremost accomplishment of the term is to distinguish being in a dynamic sense of factuality from the being that is an abstract object of thought. To adult educators accustomed to the language of the social sciences the language of German phenomenology will seem unnecessary and perhaps pretentious. I argue, however, that for all its unusualness this language holds the potential for the disclosure of exceptional meanings.

Worldview construction is prompted by the adult's search for meaning in the areas of ultimate, penultimate, and immediate personal concerns. Human beings seek meaning and intelligibility in respect to: 1) the ultimate origin and destiny of the world, and their place in the evolving cosmos, 2) broad theoretical issues related to politics, ethics, economics, law, and so forth, and 3) their own life activities, life goals, and personal relationships.

In Chapter Two the work of Hans-Georg Gadamer, professor emeritus of philosophy at the University of Heidelburg, is reviewed briefly. Gadamer, more than any other contemporary philosopher, has rehabilitated the notion of tradition. Since the Enlightenment period of intellectual history, tradition has been looked upon as an obstacle to progress. The *philosophes* of the Enlightenment were quick to see in tradition the "dead hand of the past." This prejudice exists today among those who celebrate the Enlightenment uncritically.

Tradition represents canonical experience, that is, privileged experience in terms of which all subsequent experiences are measured. Tradition forestructures understanding: tradition not only prompts us to respond to questions in a particular manner but also inclines us to prefer some questions over others. Tradition is a dynamic reality. Individuals do not simply carry out what tradition prescribes unless they are especially obtuse. Most adults in Western democratic cultures interact with their traditions. In the light of new experiences adults reinterpret tradition and retrieve old meanings of the tradition. Tradition has the power to change people; people have the power to change tradition.

Tradition influences us to make provisional judgments about our life experiences. That is, tradition gives us prejudices. In the pre-Enlightenment sense of the word, as Gadamer has pointed out, prejudice did not have a pejorative connotation. A prejudice was simply a provisional judgment that was made until further evidence could be weighed. Since no one can avoid living within a tradition of some sort, all persons have prejudices, assumptions, and beliefs about the world and themselves. Quite clearly language is a part of a person's tradition. John Dewey's observation that all experience is social and involves communication underscores the linkage of experience to language.

Worldview construction is an interpretive understanding of experience in terms of one's prejudices, assumptions, and beliefs. New experiences can be rejected on the basis of these prejudices, assumptions, or beliefs or, to the contrary, prejudices, assumptions, or beliefs can undergo change in the face of new experiences.

An analysis of knowing and thinking is undertaken in Chapter Three. Experiencing includes knowing and thinking. Knowing refers to sensory knowledge and percepts, to abstract knowledge and concepts, and to networks of memories and judgments which constitute beliefs. In this latter sense knowledge is interpreted as justified belief.

We cannot know anything purely, objectively, and with certainty. There is an absolute truth about the world but this is available only in a God's-eye view. We know things relative to our individual perspectives. There are no absolute self-justifying beliefs upon which we can ground other beliefs. There is no Archimedean point outside of the human condition by which we can leverage "pure and objective" knowledge of the world. What is proposed is essentially an antifoundationalist theory of knowledge, a kind of theory that has had a long history in Western philosophy.

Thinking and knowing are intussusceptive. Thinking involves the formation and use of percepts, concepts, judgments, and beliefs. Knowing involves thinking in that thinking connects percepts, concepts, judgments, and beliefs in such a manner that these constitute knowledge. Furthermore, thinking is not merely a purely intellectual operation. The notion of thinking includes a rich variety of operations: reflecting, introspecting, intuiting, feeling, willing, imagining, and so forth.

Thinking affects behavior and is affected by behavior; thinking affects feeling and is affected by feeling; thinking affects willing and is affected by willing. In thinking there is an experiential unity of knowing, feeling, doing, and willing. These aspects of thinking are distinct in the logical order but interpenetrative in the existential order.

Prejudices guide thinking along comfortable and familiar paths; assumptions serve as foundations or "starting blocks" for lines of reasoning; existing beliefs are normative for judging new experiences. Prejudices, assumptions, and beliefs must be examined by the worldviewer. Interpretive thinking, to be authentic, must be self-referencing.

Thinking is also construed as an inner dialogue that enables people to evaluate, to solve problems, to explicate meanings, to discover, to create, and to transcend time, i.e., thinking can be communicated and shared across generations. There are several canons for systematic thinking. Thinking must be balanced, orderly, informed, self-referencing, and productive.

Chapter Four describes understanding as the product of thinking's striving for intelligibility and meaning. Understanding is an insight that integrates experiences, ideas, judgments and beliefs into a meaningful whole. This insight, many times, arrives as an intuitional prompt. Intuitional prompts are validated not only on the basis of exact reasoning but also by norms dictated by one's esthetic sense. The notion of understanding as insight is taken from the philosphical work of Bernard Lonergan. Following Ludwig Wittengenstein, understanding is discussed as a state of mind, a process, and a power. A person's comprehensive interpretive understanding is a worldview. Various structural properties of worldviews or comprehensive interpretive understandings are identified. Worldviews may be explicit or tacit, fixed or provisional, inclusive or narrow, active or passive, critical or uncritical, discerning or myopic, other-accepting or other-disdaining (all of these are continua), and may emphasize cognitive, affective, or performative dimensions of personality.

The next chapter represents a change of pace from emphasis on theory and philosophy to emphasis on the practical steps adult educators can take to establish discussion groups which explicitly address worldview construction. Worldview construction is a naturally occurring process, but can be facilitated through educational interventions. The Participation Training design for adult education, developed by Paul Bergevin and John McKinley at Indiana University, is offered as a model for the establishment of worldview construction discussion programs. Participation Training structures participant roles and behaviors, helps adults organize discussions, and sets forth norms for group process. The adult educator is essentially a facilitator of a community of interpreters.

Chapter Six argues that there is an ethical imperative for adults to examine their worldviews, if not in a group context then at least in moments of solitude. Adults have a responsibility to themselves and to society to strive for excellence, to complete their life projects to the best of their abilities. It follows that the completion of one's life project and the creation of a self are dependent upon the periodic examination of one's interpretive understanding of the world. The evaluative analysis of one's worldview will include the examination of one's prejudices, assumptions, and beliefs.

Chapter Seven proposes that theorists in the field of adult education have recognized the association between education and worldview construction without expressly using the words worldview construction. The least that can be said is that worldview construction as an aim of adult education is not incompatible with the ideas of N.F.S. Grundtvig, Eduard Lindeman, Paul Bergevin, Jerold Apps, and Stephen Brookfield.

Adult education philosophies may be viewed along a continuum bounded by ideologies of the Right and ideologies of Left. Ideologues of the Right have an excessive love of the past. They believe all adults should be familiar with the classic wisdom of the past. They tend to paternalism and the insistence that their worldviews are normative for all. Ideologues of the Left have an excessive love of the future. They believe adults need to be liberated from their false consciousness. In order to achieve their political ends, adult educators on the Left emphasize the Marxist dogma of class struggle. They tend toward messianism and the insistence that their worldviews are normative for all.

The standard for adult educators should be impartiality in controverted issues. The worldviews of adult educators are no more privileged than the worldviews of anyone else. Adult educators, whether on the Right or the Left, have no right to invade the minds of adults. Adult educators, on the contrary, should facilitate the unveiling of truth. The notion of truth as an unveiling process is one of the key ideas of Martin Heidegger. The unveiling of the truth of the world is a participatory venture. Truth is unveiled, to the extent it can be disclosed, in the sharing of interpretations. This accomplishes the fusion of individual horizons.

The final chapter relates the ideas in this book to my previous work in the area of the theoretical foundations of adult education. The notions of liberation and empowerment are discussed vis-a-vis adult learners; a critique of so-called radical adult education is presented.

My approach to worldview construction and adult education is the approach of philosophical hermeneutics. That is, I offer interpretations of issues surrounding worldview construction and education, interpretations based on my own worldview. This should go without saying since everyone speaks out of his or her worldview. Nonetheless I mention my approach to emphasize that the following pages do not contain rigorous proofs, positivistic certainties, conclusive demonstrations of propositions, or judgments that are beyond challenge. If the truth about worldview construction and adult education is to be unveiled to any extent, it will be unveiled by the community of theorists and practitioners who stand within the adult education tradition, by a community of interpreters. I welcome the interpretations of others that support or challenge my own interpretations. My prejudices, assumptions, judgments, and beliefs require continuing examination.

As I review the manuscript I note dependence on Aristotle, Plato, Peirce, Heidegger, and Gadamer. This does not mean that my philosophy should be characterized by Aristotleian, Platonist, Peircean, Heideggerian, or Gadamerian. After a manner of speaking I have entered into a dialogue with these and other authors and have taken some of their insights as my own. I hope my interpretations are internally consistent and represent more than a fuzzy eclecticism. As a result of thinking about the insights of many others over the past few years my worldview has changed. I have experienced a turn in my thought. Today I have a greater appreciation for the place of tradition in worldview construction. My appreciation of the philosophical values of the Enlightenment remains strong; I have come to recognize, however, that some Enlightenment prejudices and assumptions need to be challenged.

I wish to thank Mary McKenzie for her support and always candid, but gentle, criticisms of my ideas. I am indebted to my colleagues at Indiana University, Travis Shipp and Keith Main. They have helped me clarify my thinking on many issues in the past fifteen or so years, chiefly during informal conversations. Over the span of years I tested some ideas with the HRD Staff at Indiana University Hospitals: Jane Kleinhans, Don Weir, Patti Lupton, Erin Gold, Donna Gildea, and Regina Morrisey. Some ideas were shaped and honed as a result of their comments. My thinking on tradition and experience was refined in a graduate seminar that included Donna Wiggs, Vivian Clevinger, Steve Bohall, Helena Masters, Sharon Thomas, Cliff Goodwin, Bob Hickey, and Bob Logsden. I am grateful to them for sharing their ideas and challenging mine. I wish to note Bob Hickey's remarkable enthusiasm for adult education research and theory. His spirit was not dampened even by the terrible illness he endured.

Appreciation is extended to the faculty of Teachers College at Ball State University. During the fall term of 1989, as Emens Visiting Professor, I presented several lectures on worldview construction and education. Faculty comments were very helpful. Obviously, not everyone mentioned above agrees with me on every issue. In fact, some of my ideas evoke opposition on important points. Much of what is valuable in the following pages is due to my conversations with others; no one mentioned in this foreword is responsible for whatever is deficient in the text. A final word of thanks goes to Cathy Taylor for her patience and professional work in preparing the typescript.

Finally, I wish to dedicate this book to all of my former teachers. My life as a student has been enriched by a large number of truly excellent teachers, more than anyone has a right to expect in one lifetime.

Chapter One

WHAT IS A WORLDVIEW?

To speak of a worldview calls to mind many meanings. The lexical definition of worldview is notable for its brevity. Worldview means contemplation of the world. In this sense contemplating the world is similar to worldviewing. In another sense a worldview can mean a system of beliefs that results from contemplating the world or from acting in the world on the basis of one's contemplations.

In common speech we sometimes refer to different kinds of worldviews. Someone is said to possess a poetic worldview, a democratic worldview, a pessimistic worldview, a Christian worldview, an accountant's worldview, and so forth. The notion of worldview becomes laden with different values depending on its adjectival modifier.

Since the notion of worldview is so complex it may be helpful to begin with some preliminary definitions. Worldview is construed in two senses. First, a worldview is a vantage point given by a person's experience from which the world may be seen and interpreted. Seeing the world does not describe the simple sighting of the physical world; "seeing" is used metaphorically to signify "experiencing" the world. There are certain limitations imposed when the visual metaphor is used to stand for experiencing. "Seeing is believing" becomes the axiom that addresses the validation of truth. What this implies is that one can trust only his or her direct experience. This norm supports and cultivates individualism over community in matters of truth and falsity. On the other hand, in oral-aural cultures "Hearing is believing." Believing involves trust in others. Despite the drawbacks of the visual metaphor, it is one with which most persons are comfortable today. In any event, a vantage point is not a physical place but a location determined by a particular time in history, a particular culture, and a person's individual orientation toward reality. A vantage point, therefore, is an historico-cultural-personal environment that provides a range of observational points, a vista, a horizon.

Second, a worldview is an interpretation of the world, an understanding of the world that arises out of reflecting on one's experience of the world, an understanding that functions to explain the world to the world-viewer and make it intelligible at least on a provisional basis. A worldview provides a person with an understanding of the world in a global sense, an understanding of some aspect or aspects of the world, and/or an understanding of the relationships of different aspects of the world to each other. A worldview may be expressed in systematic language, in art or poetry, or not expressed at all linguistically in a public forum.

WORLDVIEW AS *WELTANSCHAUUNG*

Worldview is a term that translates the German *Weltanschauung.* Arguably no philosopher has explored the subtle nuances of the notion of *Weltanschauung* more successfully than the late Martin Heidegger, even accounting for his frequent use of neologisms and a penchant for convoluted prose. Heidegger is one of the most celebrated philosophers of the twentieth century, but he is also a controversial figure. It is perhaps best to look briefly into the controversy before proceeding with some of his thoughts.

Simply put Heidegger has been accused of harboring Nazi and anti-Semitic sympathies. It has been noted, however, that he publicly rejected the crude biological racism of National Socialism. Also, it has been argued that the extent to which he cooperated with Hitler's regime was dictated by opportunism. Heidegger supposed Hitler to be a mere political manager who would help Germany fulfill its destiny as a world leader, a manager who could be easily manipulated and swayed by the logic of Germany's best professors including, of course, the celebrated Heidegger. In any event, no intrinsic connection can be made between the body of his philosophical work and any alleged pro-Nazism or anti-Semitism. It is quite possible to make use of a philosopher's insights even when the philosopher falls short of ethical ideals. Intellectual acumen is distinct from moral probity.[1]

Heidegger's explication of *Weltanschauung* or worldview is located in *The Basic Problems of Phenomenology.*[2] He underscores the fact that *Weltanschauung* is a German word and not a term derived from Greek or Latin roots. There is no word such as *kosmotheoria,* for example in Greek philosophy. His emphasis on this point is not a matter of national pride but a way of stating that the concept of *Weltanschauung,* although rooted in long-standing philosophical traditions, is essentially a modern concept related to the values of the eighteenth century Enlightenment period in Western intellectual history. In fact, the word was first used by the preeminent Enlightenment philosopher, Immanuel Kant. In its first usage the term referred to a beholding of the world, a perception of the world, an apprehension of nature in a general sense.

Both Johann Goethe and Alexander von Humboldt subsequently employed the word in Kant's sense and the meaning entered into the German language. The philosopher Friedrich Schelling, however, introduced a shift in the word's meaning. Schelling assigned the word not to sense observation but to intelligence. According to Schelling intelligence is influenced at the unconscious level through experience and, in due course, a worldview manifests itself to consciousness through a process of intuition. Thus, a worldview becomes a conscious way of apprehending and interpreting a universe of beings.

A worldview, states Heidegger, always includes a view of life. It grows out of "an all inclusive reflection on the world and the human *Dasein,* and this happens in different ways, explicitly and consciously in individuals or by appropriating an already prevalent worldview."[3] Every individual's worldview is determined by the cultural environment: folkways, lore system, race, class, and stage of culture. A worldview results from the possession of a particular horizon. In another sense, a worldview presents the observer with a particular horizon. Each individual's worldview arises out of a natural worldview, out of a range of conceptions of the world, out of a unique set of experiences, and out of the way *Dasein* is at any given time.

Dasein is the word used by Heidegger to speak of the being of being-human. The word was coined to distinguish the being of being-human from the being of animals or inanimate things. Literally the term means "being-there" but *Dasein* is seldom translated since it is so difficult, if not impossible, to render an exact meaning in another language of what Heidegger wished to convey. The mechanical substitution of alleged literal meanings for *Dasein* does not reveal what *Dasein* connotes. *Dasein* is not to be taken as a description of being-human in purely biological, psychological, sociological, or political terms (although all of these aspects of being are involved in being-human) but rather in its ontological connotation. Biological, psychological, sociological, or political dimensions of being-human are necessary but not sufficient approaches for the development of an adequate understanding of what it is to be human.

One of the best explanations of *Dasein* is the one offered by William Barrett. As a professor of philosophy Barrett talked to his students about a novel with a hero whose name was *Dasein.*[4] *Dasein* is thrown into existence and into the world out of his own nothingness, spends his life jostled by trivial talk that tries to pass for communication, and feels all the while his throwness toward extinction. Haunted by death and feeling thrust into the mouth of the void, *Dasein* attempts to work out his own authenticity. In fact, it is precisely due to his tenuous and terrible circumstances that *Dasein* is aware of the task of becoming authentic. *Dasein* is able to discover the utmost possibilities of his being only through experiencing himself as a being-in-time and a being-toward-death.

Heidegger argues that a worldview is not a matter of theoretical knowledge but instead a way of being that requires conviction if the worldview is to guide the person in times of pressure. A worldview is not the same as a philosophical speculation. There is no need to pass Philosophy 101, or even attend the course, to be able to construct a worldview. A worldview is a personal understanding, an understanding that arises out of life experience and not simply the experience of developing a conceptual system.

A worldview is forged in the trenches of life and not in the rear echelon, it is built piece by piece as one makes a way in the work-a-day world and not solely in ivory towers. A worldview is constructed amid all the vicissitudes of life, in a cauldron of laughter and tears, of sweat and pain, of harsh words, penetrating glances, and tender gestures. A worldview takes its shape, texture, and substance not in the seminar room but in the marketplace.

I am not suggesting that worldview construction must be antiphilosophical or anti-intellectual. Philosophers also have worldviews that may or may not, in the actual living of life or *lebenspraxis,* be coextensive with their philosophical systems. A worldview springs from each person's experience as this experience progressively, at variable rates of progression, unveils before the worldviewer the truth of the world and the truth of his or her existence at a particular point of the person's being-in-time. More will be said in a subsequent chapter about truth as an active process of unveiling reality through the sharing of personal interpretations of the world and the resulting fusion of individual horizons. We tend to think of truth as something other than an active collaborative process, something other than an unveiling of illusions, misconceptions, distortions, and whatever else disguises reality. Nonetheless, Heidegger's notion of truth holds much promise for understanding what we are really about when we investigate the world.

What Heidegger seems to say is that each individual essentially is required to construct a worldview by virtue of being-human. *Dasein* strives for authenticity. It is impossible to gain authenticity without commitment to a worldview. No one can avoid completely the labor associated with worldview construction by simply taking a worldview "off the rack," so to speak, and wearing it. Some try to fit themselves into a prefabricated worldview, but this is only because of *Dasein's* fallenness. Heidegger's notion of the fallenness of *Dasein,* it must be emphasized, has nothing to do with the "fall of Adam." Fallenness is not used in a negative sense but only to describe *Dasein's* being lost amid idle talk, empty curiosity, and the ambiguity that typifies everyday existence.[5]

Authenticity demands of each person the construction of a worldview. Heidegger speaks of authenticity when speaking of the ontological possibilities of *Dasein.* He does not use the term in the thin senses used in popular psychology. His prose may be heavy and terribly complicated, but he never gives himself over to psychobabble. To become authentic means to complete one's life project by actualizing the personal and situational potentials available in life, that is, by being-in-the-world fully with a commitment to pursue all opportunities for ontic realization.

Whether Heidegger's estimation of the meaning of worldview seems appropriate may be legitimately argued. It cannot be disputed, though, that anyone who undertakes a delineation of the meaning of worldview must take Heidegger's thinking into consideration. His comments about what constitutes a worldview are taken here as largely valid. This does not imply, however, that he has said the last word.

INTERPRETING THE WORLD

World refers not merely to the physical world comprised of other subjects and objects but also includes the worldviews of others, and one's own subjectivity and its contents. World is used in its broadest and most inclusive sense. Furthermore, world is employed in an intentional sense. The intentional world that is the object of worldviewing is a phenomenon at least partially constructed by the worldviewer in the very act of viewing. The world I view is partially the result of my worldview and what I bring to the world being viewed. Likewise, my worldview is partially the result of the world that is viewed. The world exists independently of my mind. The world I view, however, takes on a definite texture and coloration in that I project upon it some features in my very act of viewing or interpreting.

The world appears in human consciousness as essentially ambiguous and mysterious. The mysteriousness of the world elicits the awe or wonder that is, according to Plato, the foundation of philosophy.[6] Awe in the face of the world stimulates inquiry; inquiry is oriented toward the resolution of mystery and reduction of ambiguity. Since we cannot experience the world with a God's-eye view, we construct interpretations of the world that are limited and relative to our narrow perspectives. Any interpretation of the world, chiefly the result of thinking about experience, represents an understanding of the world that brings only a degree of satisfaction, only a tenuous explanation of the world; the mystery of the world can never be completely resolved nor can its ambiguity be reduced totally. Some interpretations of the world are more complete and more credible than others. No interpretation, however, is perfect or so attractive as to compel belief. Interpretation is the key to coming to grips with the essential character of a worldview. A review of the meaning of interpretation or hermeneutics is appropriate at this juncture.

Hermeneutics is taken from the Greek *hermeneuein* which in English is rendered as "to interpret." The Greek word points etymologically to the priestess who attended the oracle at the ancient shrine of Delphi, and to the god Hermes. It was the priestess who interpreted the rumbling sounds issuing from the shrine and made these sounds meaningful. Hermes, the Roman Mercury, was known as the messenger of the gods, a messenger who took what was beyond the ken of human knowledge and transformed it into something understandable. In the hermeneutic process, according to Richard Palmer, "something foreign, strange, separated in time, space, or experience is made familiar, present, comprehensible; something requiring representation, explanation, or translation is somehow "brought to understanding"—is interpreted.[7]

In his classic introduction to hermeneutics Palmer notes that the interpretive process has undergone definitional changes over the centuries. It is sufficient to mention here that hermeneutics applied originally to the work of those in biblical exegesis. Those who interpreted the Bible made clear what the Bible "said" for the benefit of the illiterate or nearly literate. In a largely aural-oral society it was not uncommon to depend on a small class of skilled readers to ascertain the meanings of the written word. In recent times hermeneutic methodology has been applied to the interpretation of art and symbols, and as a method in phenomenological/philosophical investigations.[8]

The process of interpretation, I maintain, is both an art and a science. This process is directed toward making the world, in its totality or separate aspects, intelligible. The world has something to "say," the world discloses messages to those who are alert to what it communicates, even when we account for the "messages" we project into the world in the act of viewing it. To express this in a different way, the world is like a text that is available for reading. Interpretation is involved in the act of reading. There is never a purely literal meaning of a text removed from the interpretive subjectivity of the reader. We can read what is "there" in the world but in the act of reading we "read into" the world meanings that reflect our personal values and previous experiences. We do not read the world as it is in itself but as it stands at the intersection between its own objectivity and our subjectivity. In experiencing the world we never capture what it is in itself, but we do grasp it sufficiently to enable us to claim that the world is not simply an artifact of our minds. We experience the world because it is there; it is there in a particular mode-of-being for each of us because we make it commensurate with the way we see. The world experienced by Scrooge prior to and after the visits of the spirits were two very different worlds. Our experience of the objective world, therefore, is always affected by our disposition and the character of our directedness toward the world.

A worldview is an interpretive understanding a person reaches after reflecting on his or her experience of the world, i.e., after thinking about the meaning of the world as it is in itself. Part of the message we "hear," of course, is projected into the world in the act of hearing. Each of us attaches meanings to the world as we experience the world in terms of our existing personal worldviews. The entire hermeneutic process aims at the disclosure of meaning. But what is meant by meaning?

MEANINGS

Different constructions can be placed on the word meaning. There are, in fact, various meanings that have been associated with the word meaning. Philip Phenix examined what he called the basic modes of human understanding and suggested there are six fundamental patterns of meaning.[9] He claimed that each of these realms of meaning is distinctive by virtue of the methods used in securing meaning, leading ideas, and characteristic structures. The first realm, symbolics, refers to language, mathematics, and nondiscursive symbolic forms such as rituals and gestures. Second, empirics refers to physical, biological, psychological, and social sciences. Meanings are expressed as probable empirical truths. Third, esthetics refers to the various arts. Meanings are associated with contemplative perception.

The fourth realm is synnoetics, a term from the Greek *synnoesis* which means meditative thought. This realm concerns personal knowledge or insight that comes from direct and concrete experience. Ethics is the fifth realm of meaning and concerns moral meanings associated with personal conduct and deliberate decisions. The sixth realm relates to meanings that are "comprehensively integrative." This area embraces history, religion, and philosophy.

The classification schema devised by Phenix manifests a variety of possible legitimate definitions of meaning. In present circumstances, however, I wish to narrow the connotative possibilities of the term so as to deal with the concept as expeditiously as possible. Meaning can refer to the purpose of something, to its worth or value, to its significance. We know the meaning of a pencil when we recognize it as a writing instrument. This elongated instrument was intended to be used for writing. I treasure a photograph of a loved one not because of its monetary value but because it helps me recall the loved one to mind. It has a special meaning for me that it does not have for a stranger. A wedding ring signifies the union of husband and wife; it says something about mutual commitment and is meaningful to the couple.

There is another sense of the term that must be examined. When a cryptographer looks at a coded message the writing appears to be gibberish. It is unintelligible; it does not make sense, it is incoherent. The message is meaningless until the cryptographer finds the key of the coded message and unlocks its meaning.

The sense in which I use meaning indicates intelligibility, worth, and coherence. Something has meaning if it satisfies, insofar as possible, the yearning to understand, to find clarity, to locate a reason for a state of affairs, to come to grips with a problem. Given these connotations I propose there are three kinds of meaning sought by human beings: 1) meaning associated with ultimate concerns, 2) meaning associated with penultimate concerns, and 3) meaning associated with personal concerns. All three of these are logically distinct but existentially interpenetrative.

Ultimate Meaning

The world presents itself to us as a mystery, something that generates a feeling of awe or wonder. Inquiry into the ultimate meaning of the world begins with this wonder. Only the very insensitive person, or someone overwhelmed by life's circumstances, has never experienced the undeciphered intuitions that come to consciousness on occasion.

The world strikes us, on a seemingly unscheduled basis, with its oddness. The world seems uncanny.[10] The sense of the world's uncanniness prompts what some philosophers have called the central question of philosophy: Why is there something instead of nothing? Indeed, when I look to myself in reflective moments I discover my essential implausibility. My existence in the twentieth century depends not only on the existence of countless ancestors in preceding centuries (if any single ancestor did not exist I would not exist) but also on the meetings, whether planned or by chance, that initially brought pairs of human beings together who somehow were attracted to one another. This intuition of personal existential implausibility only deepens when it comes to mind that each individual is the result of a particular sperm cell uniting with a particular ovum in the reproductive process. Why does something exist instead of nothing? Why do I exist instead of not existing?

Beyond the awe that heralds the advent of serious thinking about the world, and beyond being grasped by an intuition of ontological contingency framed by a sense of the oddness of the world, human beings are so constituted that anxiety is their lot. They are anxious because they realize (perhaps without being able to articulate the experience) their being is *Sein zum Tode*—being-toward-death. The same fundamental human anxiety that drives and energizes human creativity can also overpower and distract; this same dis-easement that provokes questions about meaning sometimes pushes people to the brink of darkness. The tendency to find coherence and intelligibility is one of the most powerful tendencies human beings can experience, even when they are not able to name the tendency.

The nineteenth century philosopher William Dilthey, in the words of one commentator, noted in humans "a persistent tendency to achieve a comprehensive interpretation, a *Weltanschauung,* a philosophy, in which a picture of reality is combined with a sense of its meaning and value, and with principles of action."[11] We ask about the origin of the cosmos, its purpose if it has a purpose. We seek a coherent portrayal of the world. We strive to decipher its messages that resonate in our very depths. We strive to quiet our thirst for intelligibility.[12]

Ultimate concerns may be identified chiefly with questions that are, and have been for thousands of years, at the core of religious thinking. Is God real? What is God like? What does God want of us? What is our place and purpose in this immense cosmos? Why is there physical and moral evil in the world? Why suffering? What is the meaning of human history? What is the point of the "big bang" that birthed the universe? What is the significance of the evolutionary process? The worldviews constructed in response to these questions are expressed usually in creeds, cults (worship activities), and moral codes. Sometimes these expressions are overtly religious and sometimes they are not. Beliefs, values, hopes, and ideals associated with ultimate concerns become constituent elements of worldviews.

Many ultimate concerns are investigated by philosophers who appeal for the justification of their cognitive claims not to divine authority but to natural reason, not to an initial faith in a deity but to faith in the human ability to make inferences based on extrareligious experiences. Philosophers, and others who tackle issues of ultimate concern from purely philosophical assumptions, have their own credal systems, stylized social rituals, and faith requirements as well. Usually these creeds, rituals, and faith requirements are disguised. Anyone who begins to interpret the world begins on the basis of some presuppositions that are accepted as axiomatic whether these presuppositions appear as religious or, on the other hand, as purely rational givens.

There are no pat answers to ultimate questions. No one's inferences are unshakably solid, absolutely demonstrated, and beyond challenge. The most a philosopher can do is formulate arguments that are credible. Inferences about ultimate concerns, like religious doctrines, are not provable; they can be either believed or disbelieved. The atheists's as well as the theist's interpretations are, under fine analysis, accepted on the basis of belief and not knowledge, and in relation to a commitment to a way of thinking and living. The agnostic also develops his or her inter-pretations on certain belief-assertions about the very nature of human knowledge and the limits of human understanding. Cognitive claims in both religion and philosophy require some kind of trust if they are to be affirmed and are not amenable to apodictic demonstration.

In the seventeenth century Rene Descartes, designated by many as the father of modern philosophy, maintained that philosophy begins not in wonder but in doubt. The challenge of philosophy is the overcoming of doubt through the achievement of certitude. Certitude can be gained through the use of mind and method. To attain certitude of his own exis-tence Descartes uttered his famous dictum "I think, therefore I am." Methodological thinking became the guarantor of certitude. Propositions about God, immortality, freedom and other ponderous matters, it was assumed, could be proven beyond any doubt if only the mind followed a rigorous chain of reasoning akin to reasoning of the geometrician.

Morris Berman's description of this paradigm is apt: "Man's activity as a thinking being. . . is purely mechanical. The mind is in possession of a certain method. It confronts the world as a separate object. It applies this method to the object, again and again and again, and eventually it will know all there is to know. The method, furthermore, is mechanical."[13]

The frenetic quest for absolute certainty and universal knowledge ended with the demise of nineteenth century rationalism. Only the most hidebound rationalist today would persist in the argument that issues of ultimate concern can be decided with absolute certainty through adher-ence to logical proofs. We have learned in the past hundred years or so that one problem unlocked begets a dozen mysteries, and that there are limits to human knowledge. We are not spectators of a world that is hand-ily "out there" for objective inspection; we are participants in a world that is colored by projections of our subjectivity even as we view it. We can be certain of few things. About most important and complex mat-ters all we can do is construct interpretations worthy of informed belief.

Why bother thinking about ultimate concerns if there will never be certitude, if there will never be answers, if there is nowhere to be found a yellow brick road? Perhaps no one has responded to this question with more insight than Hannah Arendt. "It is more than likely," she wrote, "that men if they were ever to lose their appetite for meaning we call thinking and cease to ask unanswerable questions, would lose not only the ability to produce those thought-things that we call art but also the very capacity to ask all the answerable questions upon which every civilization is founded."[14]

The quest for ultimate meaning seems to be constituent of the human condition. We seek answers not with any expectation that reality will become perfectly translucent or that unanswerable questions will be finally resolved, but with the assurance that the process of striving for meaning contributes to our growth as human beings and outcomes of the evolutionary process which cannot be foreseen. We shall never grasp the unreachable star, but not to reach for it imprisons us in the languor of unsearched possibilities. In any event, most human beings are incapable of shutting off their ultimate concern.

"How is it ultimately with the world?" we ask. Lacking any certain knowledge we interpret the world on the basis of experience and secure the best available understanding. But this is only one dimension, albeit a tremendously important one, of human concern.

Penultimate Concerns

Penultimate concerns embrace broad theoretical questions about a host of complex, abstract, and controversial issues. The ways in which we respond to these questions, in theory or practice, impact human interactions profoundly. It may seem at times that penultimate concerns are remote from daily life, but the answers given to many questions revolving around penultimate concerns shape the currents of ordinary life.

In the area of political thinking, for example, we ask what is the ideal way of organizing individuals into a society, we ask to what extent the body politic can be open and tolerant of diversity while maintaining order and stability, we ask whether a democratic form of government is best under all circumstances, we ask what means are politically feasible and appropriate for the advancement of the commonweal. Political theory may seem dry and abstruse until it is translated into practice. Interpretations abound in political matters because of diverse points of view and the complexity of political issues.

Political leaders of various partisan persuasions offer diverse proposals for the betterment of society. We can fairly assume that the majority of these officials have the best interests of the nation at heart, but they see things differently, emphasize different values, and engage in policy formulations with certain unavoidable biases not the least of which relates to their reelection. They have at their disposal the same facts but they interpret these facts from different perspectives and under opposing assumptions. In essence they arrive at specific political beliefs and understandings as individuals who see reality through the lens of their own experience.

Ethical issues fall under the rubric of penultimate concerns. People may agree on fundamental ethical values and principles, but the application of these principles to the concrete circumstances of life is not always easy. Two persons may agree that human life is valuable and that extraordinary or heroic measures need not be implemented to save someone who is terminally ill. One individual, though, may evaluate a particular medical intervention as an ordinary measure while the other person sees it as an extraordinary measure. Definitional problems arise over the same sets of facts and disagreement follows. Ethical principles may seem boring when these principles are discussed in a public forum, but ethical principles and their applications are directly relevant to individuals when these principles are applied to individual cases.

We may agree that justice means to give to each what is his or her due. When the time comes to divide finite resources among real people, however, we may not be sure as to what constitutes justice in the specific instance. Facts are not always interpreted in the same way, definitions are not always applied in the same way, priorities are not always assigned according to the same criteria.

Penultimate concerns are by no means limited to political and ethical issues. There is a wide range of theoretical matters that impact the way we live either directly or indirectly. Determinations of a theoretical nature often have practical consequences. Here are some representative questions prompted by penultimate concerns: What constitutes a worthwhile education? To what extent has television influenced the learning habits of children? How can the economy be managed most effectively and fairly? What percentages of the gross national product should be spent on national defense? Confronted with problems or questions in political, ethical, legal, economic, educational, and social spheres we formulate interpretations that become part of our worldviews.

Penultimate questions and answers, to be sure, are not the preserve of university professors, think tank residents, and other so-called experts. Ordinary people entertain penultimate concerns and questions; they arrive at their own interpretative answers based on their everyday experiences. Experts may be better informed on many of these issues but this does not necessarily imply greater wisdom or better responses to interpretive answers.

The interpretations most ordinary people give to penultimate questions are not contained in books or monographs; these interpretations are instantiated in their actions in the work-a-day world. Worldviews are expressed most emphatically not in books or lectures but in the way people comport themselves in the world, in the action definition they give to their being-in-the-world. It is revealing to note that the Hebrew word *dabar* can mean both word and deed.[15] A worldview statement in its most vigorous mode of expression is that which is done and not simply that which is spoken. What a person conceives to be truth is most powerful when it is done and not merely said.

The focal point of ultimate concern is infinity; the focal point of penultimate concern is more proximate to the cutting edges of life. But there is still another worldview dimension, not unrelated to the previous two, whose focal point is closest to every individual. This is the arena of immediate personal concern.

Immediate Personal Concerns

It cannot be said that everyone has experienced, for one reason or another, an awakening to ultimate concern. Nor does everyone entertain questions that arise out of penultimate concern. Every functioning adult, however, is concerned about the meaning of his or her life in the context of life goals, life activities, and interpersonal relationships. In most cases these areas of concern merge due to their close connections with each other.

From the time of childhood most people think of what they want to be when they grow up. After unrealistic considerations (a baseball player, a movie star) most people recognize more clearly their opportunities, talents, and limitations. There comes a time when illusions are dissolved. A living must be made; decisions about work and career paths must be made. Once embarked in a line of work it is not unusual to seek meaning in that work, a meaning that transcends the paycheck. Serious reflection leads to serious questions: What is the significance of my work for personal growth? What goals am I accomplishing? What is it that I want out of work? What challenges have I set for myself? Career changes frequently are made in the wake of these questions.

There comes a time in the lives of individuals when they stand back and try to gain perspective on the activities that characterize their lives. Not only is there an evaluation of one's work life but a search for meaning relating to nonwork time. Typical questions may include the following: What are the patterns of my leisure-time activities? What do these patterns tell me about myself? Should my free time be spent totally in play or should I dedicate some of my time to the service of others? Have I fallen into a rut regarding the things I do? What new activities belong in my life?

During the adult years interpersonal relationships are often studied and weighed in the balance. What is the meaning of my relationship with my parents? What is the truth of my relationship with my spouse? How should I define my relationships with my children? What relationships, if any, are poisoning my life? What can I do to strengthen and renew relationships with friends? What is the meaning of my life in terms of the entire constellation of relationships in my life?

At the bottom of this, and sometimes amid great turmoil, adults are testing their ideals, values, convictions, beliefs, opinions, feelings, fears, and hopes. They seek an interpretation of their lives that is credible, an interpretation that supplies them with an understanding of their being-in-the-world however fragile and tenuous that understanding may be.

It is difficult to imagine a functioning adult who does not possess some kind of theory of the world that is expressed in his or her daily life whether in word or deed. All adults have some kind of understanding of the intentional world, i.e., the world that enfolds their own consciousness as well as the consciousness of others. Likewise, it takes little insight to recognize the linkages that exist among ultimate, penultimate, and immediate personal concerns. These concerns interpenetrate one another. Someone's religious or philosophical beliefs will color, and be colored by, the person's thinking about ethical, political, or social issues. Similarly, how a person lives out his or her life in respect to life goals, activities, and relationships will condition, and be conditioned by, that person's ethical, political and social values, and religious or philosophical commitments. The interconnections among ultimate, penultimate, and immediate personal concerns are not always well defined since human beings are not always consistent.

How adults construct worldviews as a naturally occurring process, and how they can come together to help each other examine their worldviews, is the burden of subsequent chapters. How tradition plays its part in worldview construction is considered next.

CONCLUSION

A worldview is an interpretation of reality that provides an understanding of the world. Worldviews are constructed in response to the human being's ultimate, penultimate, and immediate personal concerns. A worldview embraces knowledge, ideas, feelings, values, assumptions, and beliefs. A worldview may be manifested either in speech or action. Worldviews are given to us, handed over to us, when we are young, and later reformulated and constructed when we reflect on experience. An analysis of the place of tradition and experience in the construction of a worldview begins in the next chapter.

REFERENCES

1. The controversy surrounding Heidegger's alleged anti-Semitism came to full fury with the publication of *Heidegger and Nazism* by Victor Farias. Translated by P. Burrell & G. Ricci. Philadelphia: Temple University Press, 1989. Michael Zimmerman characterizes the book as "vicious and at times dishonest." He also argues that no intrinsic relationship exists between Heidegger's philosophy and National Socialism. See Zimmerman's "Philosophy and Politics: The Case of Heidegger: in *Philosophy Today,* Vol. 33, No. 1/4, 1989. See also *Der Spiegel's* interview with Heidegger published after his death in *Philosophy Today,* Vol. 20, No. 4/4, 1976.
2. Heidegger, Martin. *The Problems of Phenomenology.* Translated by Albert Hofstadter. 2nd Edition. Bloomington: Indiana University Press, 1988, pp. 5–15. Hofstadter's preface, lexicon, and appendix "A Note on the Da and the Dasein" is especially helpful for understanding Heidegger's sometimes dense terminology.
3. Ibid., p. 5
4. Barrett, William. *The Illusion of Technique.* London: William Kimber, 1979, p. 233–35.
5. Heidegger, Martin. *Being and Time.* Translated by John Macquarrie and Edward Robinson. New York: Harper and Row, 1962, pp. 219–35.
6. "The sense of wonder is the mark of the philosopher. Philosophy indeed has no other origin, and he was a good genealogist who made Iris the daughter of Thaumas." That is, Iris is the goddess of the rainbow and a messenger of the gods; Thaumas is the prompter of wonder. Plato. "Theaetetus." Translated by F. M. Cornford. In *The Collected Dialogues of Plato.* Edited by Edith Hamilton & Huntington Cairns. Princeton: Princeton University Press, Seventh printing, 1973, p. 860.
7. Palmer, Richard. *Hermeneutics.* Evanston: Northwestern University Press, 1969, p. 14. Palmer's work on hermeneutics remains the best fundamental introduction published. The book reviews interpretation theory in Schleiermacher, Dilthey, Heidegger, and Gadamer and is anything if not thorough.

8. Ibid., pp. 33–45.
9. Phenix, Philip. *Realms of Meaning.* New York: McGraw–Hill, 1964, pp. 6–7. Phenix argues that the six domains of meaning in which every person needs to develop understanding and skills represent the basis for general education and curriculum development.
10. Op. cit., Heidegger, *Being and Time,* p. 233.
11. Richman, H. P. "Wilhelm Dilthey," in *The Encyclopedia of Philosophy.* Edited by Paul Edwards. New York: Macmillan, Reprint Edition, 1972, Volume 2, pp. 404–5.
12. The following comment of Etienne Gilson, Thomas Langan, and Armand Maurer further illumines Dilthey's thought: "The development of religious worldviews and the efforts of great poets have been intermingled with philosophy as part of the entire human effort that has continued, since the Greeks, to pose the questions with which we are still struggling today. By showing the close interrelation of religious and poetic worldviews with the development of philosophy, Dilthey demonstrates that the key to understanding . . . does not lie in philosophy as traditionally developed, but in the new philosophy he is proposing, the science of the spirit." In Gilson, et al. *Recent Philosophy: Hegel to the Present.* New York: Random House, 1966, p. 94.
13. Berman, Morris. *The Reenchantment of the World.* New York: Bantam: 1984, pp. 20–21.
14. Arendt, Hannah. *The Life of the Mind.* New York: Harcourt, Brace, Jovanovich, 1978, p. 62.
15. Campbell, J. Y. "Word." *A Theological Word Book of the Bible.* Edited by Alan Richardson. New York: Macmillan, 5th Printing, 1967, p. 283.

Chapter Two

WORLDVIEW CONSTRUCTION: TRADITION AND EXPERIENCE

In the opening scene of the musical *Fiddler on the Roof* the dairyman Tevya is seated on the thatched roof of a modest cottage. He plays a fiddle a short while and then speaks in explanation of his symbolic presence on the roof. Each of the villagers of Anatevka, he says, is like a fiddler on the roof. Each of the villagers tries to scratch out a tune without falling into harm. The chorus arrives on scene singing the word "Tradition."

Because of their traditions, Tevya continues, the villagers have been able to keep their balance. They have traditions for everything. Tradition controls how to eat, how to sleep, and how to wear clothes. Tevya confesses he does not know the origin of the tradition of wearing a prayer shawl but because of their traditions "everyone knows who he is and what God expects him to do." The chorus of villagers enthusiastically renders the song "Tradition."

Later in the play Tevya is hard pressed when the young tailor Motel proposes to Tevya's daughter. This violates the tradition of formal marriage arrangements made by parents and a matchmaker. The young tailor takes things into his own hands, proposes marriage, and arranges his own marriage. This shocks and scandalizes Tevya. Tradition has been violated. In the end Tevya agrees to the marriage and blesses the young couple.[1]

If there is a moral to the story it is this: Tradition is useful as a guide for conducting one's life; it helps bring balance to life and makes decision making less arduous. But in exceptional circumstances tradition must bend to permit life to be lived to its fullest. This is not a bad moral considering the pejorative sense in which tradition has been understood since the Enlightenment.

INTRODUCTION: TRADITION AS OBSTACLE

Since the very beginning of the Enlightenment, say in the latter seventeenth century, tradition has been viewed as an obstacle to human progress and as a punching bag by anyone who wished to establish credentials as a critical thinker. Prior to the Enlightenment, even during the Renaissance, antiquity was generally respected. An appeal to tradition and antiquity was frequently employed to support arguments. Awakened from their slumbers by the invention of moveable type, the adventures of explorers, and a new paradigm for what we would call the positive sciences, philosophers and writers found a stationary target for their criticisms and that target was tradition.[2]

Influential intellectuals such as Francois Arouet (Voltaire) and Denis Diderot in France, Edward Gibbon and David Hume in England, and Gotthold Lessing in Germany, to mention a few, led the attack against tradition. Absolutist political systems were deemed corrupt and oppressive. It was not long before the American and French revolutions would be launched against capricious monarchs, incompetent politicians, and political structures incapable of dealing with new challenges.

Religion was viewed as superstition and contrary to Reason. (Reason, of course, was always spelled with the capital letter). Religion also came under condemnation, with some justification, for its linkages with monarchism. A tradition of hostility against organized religion nonetheless emerged among many persons who thought of themselves as sophisticated and enlightened.

Traditional social norms were criticized. Traditional folkways were mocked as expressive of unenlightened naivete. The new science, as represented chiefly by the work of Isaac Newton, was the rage. A new era of human progress was on the horizon; the seeds of positivism were planted in fertile ground. Traditional approaches to education were attacked by Rousseau. The private ownership of property was associated with the monarchy, nobility, the ecclesiastical establishment, and the oppression of citizens by the wealthy. Serfdom was seen as a terrible moral as well as social evil. A new era was about to dawn, an era that would introduce a universal peace based on Reason and, above all, Criticism.

No doubt much of what was attacked by Enlightenment philosophers was justly and appropriately condemned. Many social, political, religious, educational, scientific, and economic traditions needed criticism and correction. Many of the valuable circumstances of twentieth century life are the direct result of the Enlightenment. It is equally true, however, that many of the horrible events that have happened in the twentieth century are attributable to the loss of traditions that kept things in balance. In their passionate crusade to be rid of the past, the "enlightened" elites, I propose, threw many babies out with the bath waters. More to the point of this chapter, the term tradition is today employed almost always in a pejorative sense, as in "the dead hand of tradition." What is traditional is often viewed as old-fashioned, behind the times, unenlightened, and unworthy of human beings. Yet there has been a defender of tradition among the ranks of important twentieth century philosophers. His name is Hans-Georg Gadamer.

THE REHABILITATION OF TRADITION

Gadamer was born in 1900 and at this writing (1990) is Professor Emeritus of Philosophy at Heidelburg University. He was influential in the development of philosophical hermeneutics, an approach to the interpretation of reality that is not confined to the tenets of rationalist doctrine, to the limits of a particular methodology, nor to the mere critique of ideology. Gadamer objects both to "method fanatics" who look only to methodology as the savior of understanding and to the "radical ideology critics" who account for the bias in every ideology except their own.[3]

For Gadamer philosophical hermeneutics is an interpretive process by which understandings of reality are achieved. These understandings are not dependent on particular scientific methods, intellect, analytic techniques, or the proof of rigorously formulated propositions. The interpretive process, on the contrary, is as much an art as a science; the interpretive process depends on imagination and insight, and on the use of language to cultivate understandings that are participatory, i.e., understandings that invite and assimilate different points of view and take these into consideration. It is only through participatory interpretation that a fusion of individual horizons is possible.

Some claims cannot be demonstrated and tested empirically; they can only be discussed, argued, and advocated until there appears a rationale for the acceptance or rejection of the claims, a rationale that will not be meaningful on a universal basis. Some persons will always choose not to "participate" in a particular understanding of some aspect of reality. Gadamer's philosophy is rich and stimulating across wide areas of investigation. What interests us presently, though, is his understanding of tradition.

Tradition as a Ground for Understanding

When we come into the world we arrive in a particular context and at a particular moment in history. Those around us speak a particular language. They express specific religious/philosophical beliefs and have preferred ways of acting socially and ethically. They share meanings and values, hopes and fears. They may or may not hold definite political views. They can be located in a particular socioeconomic segment of a population. They participate, perhaps, in a milieu defined by ethnic or national values. At birth we arrive not only in a physical place but also in a tradition that is being lived by our family members and their friends.

Gadamer hesitates to define tradition explicitly. Sometimes it seems to mean that which has been "handed over" (*traditio* = handed over) philosophically or in terms of art, literature, and so forth. Other times what is meant by tradition is not so clear, except that tradition is not to be considered something external to the individuals who live the tradition. A tradition is something that is lived out and is communicated in its being-lived-out to those who come within its circle of influence.

In his classic work on tradition Edward Shils states that tradition is anything that is handed down or transmitted from past to present. The presence of something from the past, however, does not "entail any explicit expectation that it should be accepted, appreciated, reenacted, or otherwise assimilated."[4] Tradition, according to Shils, includes materials, objects, beliefs, images of persons and events, practices, and institutions. The transmissible parts of human actions or practices are, of course, patterns and beliefs that require, recommend, regulate, permit, or prohibit certain patterns of behavior.

In learning the tradition of the significant others in our lives, particularly members of the familiy of origin during our formative years, we define ourselves and prepare ourselves for future learning and understanding. In this sense the tradition we learn or receive during our formative years is the foundation or ground for interpreting future experiences. The tradition is "always a part of us, a model or exemplar, a recognition of ourselves which our later historical judgment would hardly see as a kind of knowledge, but as the simplest preservation of tradition."[5]

Tradition as a Common Ground

Tradition, largely because it enables us with a language, serves as a basis for ongoing dialogue with others. We are able to communicate because we live in a community of shared meanings. We are able to agree or disagree with others because we know which words convey agreement and disagreement. Tradition is something to which we can appeal when we attempt to attain an understanding of something. We arrive at an understanding of this or that on the basis of a conversation with others who share the tradition. "That which has been sanctioned by tradition and custom has an authority that is nameless, and our finite historical being is marked by the fact that always the authority of what has been transmitted—and not only what is clearly grounded—has power over our attitudes and behavior."[6]

Institutions are established on the basis of tradition and we find common ground not only with our contemporaries but also continuity with those who have gone before, those who have served and been served by the institutions established by the tradition. Furthermore, we find assurance that somehow others who come after us will find a common ground with us in sharing the tradition. The tradition gives us a sense of belonging. Those who celebrate the Jewish Seder, for example, sense being-together-with those who escaped from slavery over three millenia ago and made their way to the promised land; they live in the spirit of being-together-with those who strive against oppression today; they feel a membership with those who will celebrate the Seder in the future. Tradition unites even across the centuries and beyond the deaths of individuals.

Tradition as A Dynamic Reality

When most people think of tradition they imagine a body of dusty rules and out-of-date suppositions. Living within a tradition, according to Gadamer, has nothing to do with blind adherence to something authoritatively given. The authority possessed by a tradition is not unchallengeable; it is open to change. Living within a particular tradition an individual may "argue" with the tradition because of his or her experiences, experiences that may have never before been accounted for by the tradition. The tradition is corrected in successive generations; the tradition is reinterpreted; old meanings are retrieved, revitalized, and renewed. The tradition has power to change the lives of individuals but individuals have the power to change the tradition. Respect is paid to tradition not simply by following its dictates blindly but by taking it seriously enough to enter into a dialogue, so to speak, with the tradition.

Persons do not define themselves merely by "naming" their traditions, as if a tradition is only an external label. To say "I am an American of Polish descent, a Catholic, a Democrat, and a middle-class midwesterner" or "I am an American of Scotch-Irish ancestry, a Presbyterian, a Republican, and an upper middle-class easterner" is merely a recital of demographic data and not a vital and ongoing interaction with a tradition. A person is not solely defined by a tradition but instead works out his or her definition in terms of a dynamic interaction with tradition.

No one can outrun tradition. That you cannot go home again, as Thomas Wolfe observed, may be true. It is also true that you can never leave home. New experiences are as the layers of an onion that cover over and hide the experiences of our formative years, but once hidden the experiences of our formative years continue to exert their influence on our lives. A person defines self in terms of a tradition, whether that tradition is accepted or rejected. The tradition is continually defined and redefined by those who accept, reject, and reinterpret the tradition. Just as each individual changes during the course of life, all traditions change (sometimes imperceptibly) during the course of history.

Tradition as a Forestructure for Understanding

In order to understand how tradition forestructures human understanding it is necessary to examine another key concept in Gadamer's writing. The concept of prejudice acquired a negative connotation only in the past two hundred years. "Actually prejudice means a judgment that is given before all the elements that determine a situation have been finally examined. In German legal terminology a prejudice is a provisional legal verdict before the final verdict is reached."[7] With the Enlightenment period in the history of philosophy the notion of prejudice was viewed as the judgment forthcoming from any kind of authority, particularly the authority of tradition and the authority of the past. Former imperfect ideas were to be replaced with a perfection based on Reason once the slate was wiped clean. Reason alone was to be the arbiter, a Reason that was pristine in its goodness and keen of sight.

Yet there is no Reason independent of reasoning human beings, and reasoning human beings are no less likely to be prejudiced for their modernity. Reasoning human beings are not always reasonable; they are not capable of perfect objective judgment. Judgment, in fact, is a subjective activity. Every judgment is the act of a judging subject; there is no way to avoid subjectivity in judgment. One may hold to objective criteria in making a judgment, in order to keep the judgment fair, but to remove every aspect of subjectivity from the act of judgment is a contradiction in terms. Every human subject, in turn, is prejudiced to some extent by his or her tradition and previous experience. There is little to fear from someone who recognizes this fact of life and struggles to be fair; there is much to fear from the individual who believes he or she is preserved from every taint of conscious or hidden influences antecedent to the process of reasoning and the act of judgment.

That there is such a thing as a pure, objective framework from which subjective assessments of reality can be critiqued was the cause of serious disputation between Gadamer and the social theorist Jurgen Habermas. Habermas argues, in effect, that it is possible to stand outside of one's subjectivity, prejudices, and ideology in order to pass judgment on social actions. "Social actions can only be comprehended in an objective framework that is constituted conjointly by language, labor and domination."[8] Habermas evidently supposes that his neo-Marxist ideology is the pure and objective measure that constitutes all competing ideologies as false. "Despite his significant differences from the positivists, Habermas is, like them," writes Susan Hekman, "positing a form of objectivity for the social sciences and, like the Enlightenment thinkers, relying on the distinction between pure and impure knowledge." Hekman goes on to conclude that given the objectivist and materialist basis of Marx's work it would be improbable that someone in the Marxist tradition such as Habermas would depart substantially from a variation of the Marxist position.[9] I must subscribe to Gadamer's view. It seems peculiar to me that anyone would claim to have access to a privileged kind of knowing that transcends the subjectivity, and prejudices, of the knowing subject.

Prejudice is a provisional judgment, an inclination, a penchant for viewing things in a particular way. It is a tendency to respond to certain events in terms of patterns imposed by tradition and previous experiences. So universal is prejudice, in the pre-Enlightenment sense, that only a person without tradition and devoid of experience can claim to be totally unprejudiced. Tradition establishes patterns of preferred thought and behavior to enable people to respond to situations without taking the time to re-think in precise detail what the appropriate response should be. If the tradition has also inculcated the values of fairness and respect for others, there is little likelihood that the prejudiced response (in the modern sense of the word) will be just or malicious.

Prejudice, in the pre-Enlightenment sense, forestructures understanding and inclines a person to interpret things from the vantage point sanctioned by tradition and in accordance with the values of the tradition. "Prejudices are not necessarily unjustified and erroneous, so that they inevitably distort the truth. In fact, the historicity of our existence entails that prejudices, in the literal sense of the word, constitute the initial directedness of our whole ability to experience."[10]

Nonetheless, prejudices can be unjustified and erroneous. Tradition and experience can equip a person with prejudices that are cruel, wrongheaded, and otherwise unacceptable. It is here where skillful interpretation and participatory understanding come into play. In the "game" of interpreting together with others, it is always everyone's "turn" to interpret. And "the process of interpretation takes place whenever we 'understand,' especially when we see through prejudices or tear away the pretenses that hide reality."[11]

In the interpretation of any present situation, in the interpretive understanding of questions deriving from any present concern, the past
intrudes and shapes the ways we perceive and understand. Tradition
(and whether we react positively or negatively with a tradition) not only
influences our answers to questions but prompts the kinds of questions
we ask. As Heidegger notes, the human being is also a being-in-time,
someone who is caught within the momentum of history's flow and not
someone who stands aloof from time and history.[12] What we bring to the
experiencing of anything is as important as the event that is itself being
experienced.

TRADITION AND EXPERIENCE

Is tradition over and above experience? How does experience differ
from tradition? What kind of clarifying distinctions, if any, can be made
between tradition and experience? Is the notion of experience any less
ambiguous than the idea of tradition? These questions must be approached with a great deal of care if the functions of tradition and experience in the process of worldview construction are to be understood. It is
helpful, then, to draw out some of the meanings that attach to the concept of experience.

An Understanding of Experience

Experience is a slippery concept because it is freighted with many different connotations. No one has made this more evident than Charles S.
Peirce, a philosopher whose work had great impact on the thinking of
John Dewey. According to Peirce there are three modes of being: 1) the
being of positive qualitative possibility, 2) the being of actual fact, and 3)
the being of law that governs facts. These modes of being he called,
respectively, Firstness, Secondness, and Thirdness. Our experiences of
reality differ in relation to the three modes of being that are experienced.

The redness of an object, for example, is a positive possibility in the
sense that "before anything in the universe was yet red. . . " redness was
a positive qualitative possibility.[13] Firstness is attributed to external
objects. Wherever we find a phenomenon there is a quality to be found,
so much so that we could suppose there is nothing to a phenomenon
except its qualities. Positive qualitative possibilities, however, are not to
be identified with outward objects. Indeed, some of these qualitative possibilities, not having been actualized (not moved from potentiality to
actuality) cannot be known. We know Firstness only when instances of
Firstness are actualized in external objects.

Secondness refers to facts that resist, at least in some way, our wills. Facts are proverbally called "brutal" for a good reason. Facts possess qualities but they resist us and produce reactions in us. Mere qualities, continues Peirce, cannot produce reactions; they remain possibilities that are known as such only when they are actualized in a fact.

Thirdness consists of laws when we contemplate them from the outside only "but which when we see both sides of the shield we call thoughts. Thoughts are neither qualities nor facts."[14] Just as qualities require facts so that qualities move from potency to act, so also do facts require thought before a collection of facts becomes a law. What establishes coherent relationships among the facts in a collection, after all, is mind.

Peirce describes experience, then, not simply as sense impressions, but includes the life of thought. Inquiring, expecting, predicting, and inferring are forms of experience. The cognition of change is an experience, a passing feeling is a rudimentary fragment of experience; in essence whatever is the subject of thought and reflection can be experienced. What is remembered is experienced. "By experience must be understood the entire mental product." Even hallucinations, delusions, superstitious imaginations, and fallacies of all kinds are experiences, but experiences misunderstood; while to say that our knowledge relates merely to sense-perception is to say that we can know nothing—not even mistakenly—about higher matters, as honor, aspirations, and love."[15]

Peirce also recognized the importance of language, society, and communication for experience. It was Dewey, however, who emphasized the fundamental place of experience in education and the social character of experience. "All human experience," he wrote, "is ultimately social: that is, it involves contact and communication."[16] Again, Dewey stated, "An experience is always what it is because of a transaction taking place between an individual and what, at the time, constitutes his environment, whether the latter consists of persons with whom he is talking about some topic or event, the subject talked about being a part of the situation; or the toys with which he is playing; the book he is reading. . . or the materials of an experiment he is performing."[17]

Even the solitary person working on a particular project and in contact with various materials is linked to other persons by virtue of thought and language. The solitary individual thinks about the project. Because of the close connection between language and thought it is not unreasonable to assume the individual would not be able to think without possessing language abilities, and language is a system of communication developed by at least two people. The very nature of human experience is such that it is intimately related to thought and language, and to the matrix of community out of which language emerged.

I agree, then, that experience includes "the whole mental product." The process of experiencing results in concepts, judgments, feelings, hopes, ideals, intuitions, and so forth. Some experiences can be central to a person's life or peripheral; some experiences can lead to dramatic change or no change at all; some experiences can be integrated with previous experiences or simply shrugged off.[18] Experience, I concur, has a social dimension; in examining this social dimension we can discover that tradition is a special kind of experiencing.

Tradition is a kind of experience. Tradition is not primarily something that is described and catalogued by cultural anthropologists; it is not something categorized by social scientists. Tradition, in its foremost meaning, is something that is lived. It is a special kind of lived experience, an experience that occurs precisely because of a special social milieu. What is "handed over" in tradition is not so much a body of knowledge, a list of values, or a written inventory of ideals but instead a particular style of comporting oneself in life, a distinctive way of possessing and living out one's being-in-the-world. Nothing exemplifies the essential concreteness and existentiality of tradition more than language for we learn our mother tongue spontaneously and not by studying its grammar.

A child does not learn language in the home the same way he or she learns subject matters in school. Some teaching of language, of course, is obvious when parents play with their babies. Language, however, is largely "caught" instead of being taught. We learn to speak by participating in the flow of this special experience we call tradition. To become caught up in this flow of tradition is to be carried along a current of being-in-the-world that is reflected everywhere we look in our formative years, especially the years before socialization begins at school age. While language is perhaps the best example of the assimilation of tradition, during our formative years we master many other things because we participate in tradition.

Tradition is a special kind of experience because of its priority in time and the power of its shaping influences. In a family of origin the first experiences of a child are mediated by the modes of being of parents, grandparents, brothers and sisters, relatives and friends, modes of being that are generally similar and commensurate with an overall familial pattern. The modes of being-in-the-world of these individuals, which modes themselves were formed in part by a specific constellation of historico-environmental and genetic factors, exert a powerful influence over the child and constitute the only "world" in which the child participates from its earliest moments of focused consciousness. The early influences that help us as we struggle to define ourselves, while not insuperable, are relatively strong during the course of life.

Tradition derives its power not only because its force is initial in time but also because of the bonding that ordinarily occurs in the family of origin. Learning in the family of origin, and subsequently within the sanctioned sociocultural milieu, is reinforced because the child or youth may enjoy loving relationships with other family members and members of ethnic, national, or religious communities approved by the parents. The factors that contribute to the development of any person are myriad and almost impossible to measure. It is not unreasonable to assume, however, that a child who learns to act in a particular way from the example of parents, brothers and sisters, relatives and friends, and others who stand in a loving, supportive relationship, is more likely to act in the same way later in life than the child reared by adults who were uncaring and nonsupportive.

Tradition is to subsequent experience what the bending of the proverbial twig is to the remaining growth of the tree. The simile is not exact but accurate enough to show that tradition is foundational experience, the kind of experience that orients a person and provides a certain directedness to life. Tradition is usually the norm by which subsequent experiences are assessed; tradition may be seen as a privileged experience. All present experiences are interpreted in the light of previous experience, and especially in the light of tradition. Does this mean, then, that tradition controls and determines the course of life: Does it imply that tradition, as a special kind of experience, will always overcome experiences that conflict with tradition? At what point in the course of the lifespan does tradition fade and new experiences become more vivid in respect to their impact on a worldview?

It could happen in an individual instance that tradition would control and determine the course of an entire life. Such a scenario, however, is highly improbable. While tradition is foundational it is not causative; it exerts not absolute influence but influence relative to other life variables; tradition may incline a person in this or that direction but tradition does not deprive a person of choice. I reject as extreme and simplistic any thesis of environmental determinism. Meaning is something that is born in the interaction of a person and his or her environment; it is neither imposed from without or dictated from within the interiority of the individual.

It may also happen, for example, that a value emphasized by tradition is later mitigated or even dismissed in the face of experiences that conflict with the tradition. And while tradition is something that a person can never completely outrun, there can come a point in the lifespan where the tradition is almost completely transformed by new experiences. There are such things as total "conversions." The term conversion is usually referenced to religious conversion, but it can also apply to lifestyle, politics, and any other aspect of human life.

A child views a special world in his or her family of origin. This world changes as the child enters school and meets different people. Exposure to others opens up new vistas on new worlds. During adolescence and later on in life, the person encounters multiple viewpoints either in theory or instanced in the life practices of others: new vantage points for viewing an even more complex world are made available. Tradition, the initial life experience in terms of which all subsequent experiences are interpreted, may gradually lose its force in a substantial way. Traces of tradition, however, will always remain. It could also happen, of course, that tradition would become more influential over the lifespan even when confronted by powerful contradicting new experiences.

WORLDVIEW CONSTRUCTION AND EXPERIENCE

Permit me to expand the description of worldview previously offered. A worldview is an interpretive understanding of the world that is based on experience. Worldview construction is a process that is coterminous with experiencing the world through the lifespan. Each new experience is organized and interpreted in relation to the existing worldview. As a result the new experience can be rejected as meaningless or accepted as meaningful either totally or in part. If the new experience is accepted, it is assimilated into the existing worldview. Likewise, the existing worldview is re-organized and re-interpreted in the light of new experience. Worldviews never remain the same; they are altered—if only imperceptibly and gradually—with the arrival of each new experience.

There are no hard and fast rules governing worldview construction. Each worldview is constructed according to its own idiom. Worldviews can undergo progress or regress, expansion or contraction, renewal or decadence. Worldview construction is a process that enfolds many variables, not the least of which is the intentionality and choice of the worldviewer, to the extent the worldviewer is capable of exercising choice. While the process of worldview construction cannot be described in fine detail, some insight into the process can be attained by resorting to Jacques Derrida's notion of deconstruction.

Worldview Construction as Deconstruction

Jacques Derrida is professor of philosophy at the *Ecole Normale Superieure* in Paris. He is best known perhaps for his ideas on deconstruction. Derrida followed Heidegger in developing a critique of Western metaphysics and the language of traditional philosophy as well as everyday language. His insights are most notably evident in the field of literary criticism. Derrida claims that Western thought has been structured in terms of dichotomies or polarities: good versus evil, being versus nothingness, truth versus error, mind versus matter, and so forth. In his critiques of language he attempts to remedy these "faults." He also attends to the privileging of the spoken word over the written word in Western culture.

Deconstruction assumes that any text has no real meaning apart from the actual reading of the text by a particular individual in particular circumstance. For this reason it is sometimes claimed that deconstruction as a technique is a tool of nihilism and the destruction of meaning. Derrida, however, claims that deconstruction is "affirmation rather than questioning, in a sense which is not positive. . . I think that deconstruction is affirmative rather than questioning; this affirmation goes through some radical questioning, but it is not questioning in the final analysis."[19]

Perhaps the best explanation of deconstruction is the one offered by Barbara Johnson, the translator of Derrida's *Dissemination*. Deconstruction is not, she states, a form of literary vandalism. ". . . the word 'deconstruction' is closely related not to the word 'destruction' but to 'undo'—a virtual synonym for 'to deconstruct.'"[20] Johnson notes that the deconstruction of a text is not carried out with random doubt or skepticism but by teasing out the warring forces of signification within the text. What is destroyed in the deconstruction of a text is not the meaning of the text but the assumption that one kind of signifying should dominate all other significations.

The clever, and occasionally profound, insights of Derrida are often hidden in his sometimes unusual style of writing. It does not serve present purposes, however, to examine his philosophy but only to introduce him as the originator of the notion of deconstruction. I suggest that this notion, used originally to describe the criticism of texts, can be employed profitably in the sense of the deconstruction or critical analysis of experience. The deconstruction of experience, I note, implies not only the analysis of experience but also the destruction of selected meanings of experience. (I would argue also that some sort of destruction of textual meaning is implied in Derrida's sense of the term, but this does not hold any direct relevance to present concerns).

At any given point a person maintains a worldview, an interpretive understanding of the world. This understanding is the consequence of the individual's previous experience. Any new experience, by definition, will be different from the experiences out of which the existing worldview has been constructed. I propose that each new experience is deconstructed: each new experience is pulled apart in a way so natural and common that we seldom advert to the deconstructive operation.

We pull apart, analyze, each new experience and determine the degree to which it is compatible with the existing worldview. If compatible, or at least not contradictory or unimaginable/impossible in terms of the existing worldview, the new experience is assimilated and integrated into the existing worldview. Some new experiences, of course, are so marginally important to the worldviewer that they are virtually ignored, so to speak, at first glance.

Suppose that a new experience, though, is of such a quality and such weight that it cannot be ignored. The new experience is truly novel and somehow requires adjustment before it can be assimilated into the existing worldview. In these circumstances the deconstruction of the new experience will be more apparent to the worldviewer. The new experience needs tailoring so it can be fit into the existing worldview.

Finally, suppose a new experience represents a substantive contradiction to the existing worldview. The experience transcends anything held imaginable/possible by the existing worldview. In this case the need for the deconstruction of the new experience is obvious and the worldviewer becomes alert to the deconstructive process.

New experiences are deconstructed but so also are existing worldviews. A new experience is precisely "new" only in respect to a worldview, therefore, worldview construction occurs simultaneously with the deconstruction of each new experience. When the new experience is highly compatible with the existing worldview, the worldviewer is hardly aware of the deconstructive operation. When the new experience contradicts the existing worldview in a particularly dramatic manner, the worldviewer may become painfully aware of the deconstructive operation in relation to the existing worldview.

Some examples may elucidate the foregoing statements. During the course of an ordinary day a person greets new experiences that are compatible with his worldview. The new experiences are taken into the existing worldview.

On another day the same individual attends his first statistics class and concludes, based on previous experience, that he will never master the strange formulas in the book. During the class period he reads and begins to deconstruct the situation. The teacher seems capable. She is pleasant and her explanations are clear. She encourages the students and urges them not to be anxious about the course. At the same time he deconstructs the previous experiences that led him to believe he will fail. As a result of the deconstruction of previous experience, he changes his worldview. Deconstruction took place on two fronts: 1) in respect to the new experience, 2) in respect to the previous experiences upon which the worldview was based.

A final example: a student enrolls in a course in biology and studies evolution seriously. Evolution contradicts her worldview since the worldview includes as truth the so-called literal teaching of Genesis. She begins to feel she has "lost" her religious faith. The deconstruction of the new experience did not result in a tailoring of the new experience sufficient to fit it into her existing worldview; the deconstruction of the existing worldview revealed that it was lacking. She discusses the situation with a friend. The friend assures her that metaphor can "contain" and express truth, and that evolution is not incompatible with a religious worldview. Under further deconstruction her worldview changes. New learnings and new experiences are incorporated into her altered worldview. Of course, the student could have denied evolution or rejected her religious belief totally. Deconstruction does not assure happy endings to stories.

Deconstruction, in the sense used here, is a form of interpretation that addresses contradictions, dissimilarities, and polarities between an existing worldview and new experiences. It asks what is significant, meaningful, or truthful about new experiences; it also reviews one's existing worldview in terms of its significance, meaning, and truth claims. The examples suggest that deconstruction is scientific, systematic, and intellectual. This is not necessarily so. As a kind of interpretation deconstruction is as artful as it is scientific, and conducted on the grounds of insight as often as on the basis of logic.

Deconstruction and Reconstruction

Those familiar with the literature of the philosophy of education will have reckoned with the notion of deconstruction in light of John Dewey's concept of the reconstruction of experience. What is the difference between the deconstruction and the reconstruction of experience?

Dewey defined education as "that reconstruction or reorganization of experience which adds to the meaning of experience, and which increases ability to direct the course of subsequent experience."[21] Dewey's concept of reconstruction, I suggest, points to ideas of formation, growth, and the development of social capacity; these ideas are prominent in the textual context in which he discussed reconstruction. Formation refers to the formation of the mind through the use of appropriate materials. "The formation of mind is wholly a matter of the presentation of the proper educational materials."[22] Furthermore, formation is concerned with the formal steps of teaching methodology. As an outcome of reconstruction the individual becomes better able to profit from additional experiences. Finally, the reconstruction of experience leads ideally to a person's ability to function in society and to participate in democratic processes.

Deconstruction is used here to denote a process that occurs outside of educational settings, although educational strategies can be developed to help learners develop their worldviews. Deconstruction refers also to the critical evaluation of experiences, and to the analysis, and *pari passu* the destruction, of meanings by a worldviewer. Lastly, deconstruction as used here relates to hermeneutics, to the construction of an interpretive understanding of the world in the broadest and most inclusive sense of the term.

There may be similarities between the reconstruction and deconstruction of experience but these similarities seem insignificant when compared with differences. This is not to state that the notion of reconstruction is somehow lacking; it is merely to indicate that the two notions emphasize different meanings and serve different purposes.

CONCLUSION

Since the Enlightenment the idea of tradition has been charged, not completely unfairly, with various offenses against humankind. Tradition has been seen as the dead hand that holds back progress. Tradition, however, is an essential element in human history and in each person's individual history. Hans-Georg Gadamer has shown the positive sides of tradition and has come to be known as the great rehabilitator of the notion of tradition.

Tradition is a special kind of experience. Tradition is a canonical kind of experience, a privileged experience by virtue of its temporal priority in each of our lives and also by virtue of the fact that those who "hand over" tradition are usually loved or otherwise highly regarded.

Experience is defined as any kind of mental product, usually resulting from the interaction of an individual with the external environment. Experience is much more than sense experience. It includes thinking, feeling, intuiting, remembering, and so forth. A worldview or interpretive understanding of the world results from experience. Each new experience is analyzed or deconstructed in terms of a person's worldview; a worldview is analyzed or deconstructed in terms of new experiences. Worldview change is attributed to the deconstruction process, a process that occurs on an informal and natural basis as well as formally.

Deconstruction, in turn, is carried out by thinking about experience. In the next chapter we examine the meaning of thinking, an operation which is itself an experience or, more accurately, a reflective experiencing of experience.

REFERENCES

1. Stein, Joseph and Harnick, Sheldon. "Fiddler on the Roof." In *Ten Great Musicals of the American Theatre.* Edited by Stanley Richards. Radnor, Pennsylvania: Chilton, 1973. pp. 392ff.

2. Peter Gay's two volume *The Enlightenment: An Interpretation* remains the most lucid and readable treatment of this revolutionary period in the history of philosophy. The volumes were published by Alfred A. Knopf, New York, in 1969. For another interpretation of the Enlightenment looking backward from the French Revolution, see Simon Schama's *Citizens: A Chronicle of the French Revolution.* New York: Alfred A. Knopf, 1989. Schama maintains the ruling elite from king downward were less obsessed with tradition than with novelty. It was not so much a hatred of tradition that led to revolutionary excesses as an infatuation with change.

3. Gadamer, Hans-Georg. *Philosophical Apprenticeships.* Translated by Robert B. Sullivan. Cambridge: MIT press, 1985, p. 177.

4. Shils, Edward. *Tradition.* Chicago: University of Chicago Press, 1981, p. 12.

5. Gadamer, Hans-Georg. *Truth and Method.* Translation copyrighted by Sheed and Ward, Ltd. New York: Crossroad Publishing company, 1986, p. 250.

6. Ibid., p. 249.

7. Ibid., p. 240.

8. Habermas, Jurgen. "A Review of Gadamer's Truth and Method," in F. Dallmayr and T. McCarthy (eds.) *Understanding and Social Inquiry.* Notre Dame: University of Notre Dame Press, 1977, p. 335.

9. Hekman, Susan. *Hermeneutics and the Sociology of Knowledge.* Notre Dame: University of Notre Dame Press, 1986, p. 38. For a fuller treatment of this point see Thomas McCarthy's *The Critical Theory of Jurgen Habermas.* Cambridge, MA: MIT Press, Sixth Printing, 1988, pp. 187–93.

10. Gadamer, Hans-Georg. *Philosophical Hermeneutics.* Translated by David E. Linge. Berkeley: University of California Press, 1977, p. 9.

11. Ibid., p. 32.

12. See Heidegger's treatment of being-in-time as a basic structural mode of *Dasein* in Part Two of *The Basic Problems of Phenomenology.* Translated by Albert Hofstadler. Bloomington: Indiana University Press, Midland Book Edition, 1988, pp. 227–318.

13. Peirce, Charles S. *Philosophical Writings of Peirce.* Edited by Justus Buchler. New York: Dover Publications, 1955, p. 76.

14. Ibid., p. 78.

15. Ibid., p. 377.

16. Dewey, John. *Experience and Education.* New York: Collier Books, 15th printing, 1972, p. 38.

17. Ibid., pp. 43–44.

18. On this point see the article by Peter Jarvis, "Meaningful and Meaningless Experience: Towards an Analysis of Learning from Life." *Adult Education Quarterly,* Vol. 37, No. 3, 1987, pp. 170–71.

19. Derrida, Jacques. Quoted in Imre Salusinszky's *Criticism in Society.* New York: Methuen, 1987, p. 9. Those interested in how Derrida's work relates to hermeneutics may wish to read John D. Caputo's *Radical Hermeneutics: Repetition, Deconstruction, and the Hermeneutic Project.* Bloomington: Indiana University Press, 1987. Derrida has, like Heidegger, come under suspicion because of the recently discovered Nazi activities of his colleague Paul de Man, a leading literary critic at Yale until his recent death. While I am not inclined to agree with the substance of Derrida's philosophy, I would argue strenuously that he should not be blamed for the views of an associate. Guilt by association should have died long ago.

20. Johnson, Barbara. In her translator's introduction to Jacques Derrida's *Dissemination.* Chicago: University of Chicago Press, 1981, p. xiv. For an excellent brief summary of Derrida's work see Alexander Nehamas' "Truth and Consequences" in *The New Republic,* Vol. 197, No. 14, October 4, 1987, pp. 31–36.

21. Dewey, John. *Democracy and Education.* New York: The Free Press, 1st Freepress Paperback Edition, 1966, p. 76.

22. Ibid., p. 70.

Chapter Three

WORLDVIEW CONSTRUCTION: KNOWING AND THINKING

A worldview is an understanding of the intentional world based on the interpretation of one's experience. Experience is any mental product resulting from an interaction of a person with the world that exists independently of the individual's mind. Experience also refers to the interaction of ideas and judgments within a person's mind; these ideas or concepts originated in the individual's perceptions of the external world. In the previous chapter attention was directed to worldview construction in terms of tradition (something that might be called canonical experience or privileged experience by which all other experience is measured) and in terms of new experiences other than tradition. New experiences are interpreted in the light of a person's tradition but at the same time these new experiences impact tradition and open tradition for reinterpretation and reframing. In the present chapter the analysis of worldview construction continues by directing attention to the experience of knowing, thinking, and understanding.

INTRODUCTION: A DISCLAIMER

I wish explicitly to specify the meaning of experience to include knowing, thinking, and understanding. (Experience considered as knowing and thinking is discussed in this chapter; experience as understanding is examined in the next chapter). Prior to this, however, I must state a disclaimer: our knowledge of knowing, our thinking about thinking, and our understanding of understanding will necessarily be limited, subjective, and approximate. I mention this not as some sort of apology or excuse but as a statement of the human condition vis-a-vis knowing, thinking, and understanding. There is no purely objective Archimedean point somewhere beyond the human condition that provides leverage for the exact weighing of knowing, thinking, and understanding. Whatever is said of these operations is said by way of interpretation and by way of stipulative definition only. There is no wide consensus on the denotations of the words knowing, thinking, and understanding, but stipulative definitions function as provisional bases for further investigations.

Imagine an immense panoramic tapestry that portrays people engaged in a variety of activities and enterprises. The tapestry is mounted on huge rollers and is being wound up as a spool of film in a camera. Imagine further, for the sake of the thought experiment, that the figures of the people woven into the tapestry are thinking beings. One of the figures at the center of the scene is depicted looking off into the distance. He thinks these thoughts: "What am I doing here in this arrangement of relationships with other figures? What is the ultimate and total meaning of the actions in which all of us are engaged? I cannot see off to the far left of the tapestry; I depend on others to tell me what has already taken place and rolled on to the spool. I cannot see off to the far right of the tapestry where more of the cloth is being played out. I depend on others to tell me what they hope or fear is being unrolled. What I really need is to get outside of this tapestry to view it from a distance so as to gain perspective. How will I ever be able to see the complete meaning of the scene on this tapestry unless I get outside of it?"

The predicament of the figure woven into the tapestry is akin to the human predicament. We cannot get outside of the world to view it from a distance; we cannot gain a perspective that makes certainty possible. I cannot get outside of my own acts of knowing to evaluate thinking or understanding to be able to describe thinking or understanding with rigorous detail and exact precision.

Another problem associated with the analysis of knowing, thinking, and understanding is the fact that each of these words is freighted with a multitude of connotations and usages. Epistemology is the study of the nature and limits of human knowledge. What makes epistemological writings so difficult to understand at times is the ambiguity that surrounds key concepts. It is necessary, nonetheless, to discuss these concepts and operations at least in outline form to develop a view of how knowing, thinking, and understanding are related to the process of worldview construction.

KNOWLEDGE

There are three principal meanings, I suggest, associated with the notion of knowledge. First, knowledge can be construed in its most basic form as the consciousness that results from the reception of sensory stimuli that appear in the mind as percepts. Second, knowledge can be described in terms of cognitive consciousness, a consciousness of ideas or concepts. Third, knowledge can be apprised as an assemblage of judgments that constitute beliefs held by the knower. These beliefs reside in memory in such a manner that an individual is said to be knowledgeable or a knowing person. These three meanings do not exhaust the possible connotations of the term but serve as a framework for exploring the meaning of knowledge in a systematic way.

Knowledge: Sensate Consciousness

In the first instance knowledge refers to sensate consciousness. Sensory knowledge is the immediate apprehension of sense stimuli. These stimuli activate nerve impulses which are conducted to the cerebral cortex. The knower perceives an external reality. That is, a percept of an external reality is formed. A percept is always particular and concrete as distinct from a concept which is always universal and abstract. Sensory knowledge is a consequence of being a living organism composed of cells, tissues, and a central nervous system.

Robert Augros and George Stanciu point out that the materialist philosophy of the nineteenth century led scientists to believe that if "an external stimulus causes a change in a sense organ, that organ's response is dictated by the kind of matter the organ is made of and by the organ's structure."[1] It follows logically from this that what sense perception provides is not information about the real world but rather data about the sense organ. While we may assume a real world exists "out there" we can never really experience this world in itself. We experience merely our sensations of the world.

The authors go on to note that modern science suggests knowledge is a fact about both knower and object known. "When a man steps onto a scale that registers '187,' that '187' is a fact about both the man and the scale."[2] The separation of the subjective and objective orders, they claim, is not a part of the scientific method. Sense perception provides knowledge not only about the sense organ and how it is structured but about the sense organ's relationship with stimuli that exist independently of the human mind.

Included in the category of sensory experience is the proprioceptive sense, i.e., the sense of the extension of one's own body in space and time. As a first-year philosophy student and member of a study circle I remember our attempts to "prove" that we actually existed. The efforts, of course, were fruitless. The fact of one's own existence is a given of the proprioceptive sense. It is impossible to enlighten a sunny day by shining a flashlight at the sun just as it is impossible to prove the obvious. Descartes was wrong when he said "I think, therefore, I am." He would have done better had he stated "I sit, therefore, I am." On the other hand, his attempt to prove his own existence as a starting point for a philosophical system can be seen now as questionable at least.

Knowledge: Cognitive Consciousness

In another basic sense knowledge is the result of being conscious of an abstract object of consciousness, an idea or concept. This abstract object of consciousness differs from the object of consciousness involving the sensing of palpable realities. Percepts represent what is concrete and particular: this apple is in my hand. Concepts represent what is abstract and universal: appleness is an attribute of this object in my hand.

There is another way of expressing this: There are two levels of consciousness. Sensory experience furnishes, so to speak, the mind with percepts; the level of epistemic experience furnishes consciousness with the wherewithal for its conceptual operations. These levels, furthermore, are completely "in touch" with one another. Not all percepts, however, lead to the formulation of concepts. Just as one of the functions of sensation is the screening of stimuli (otherwise we would go awry with sensory overload), one of the functions of epistemic consciousness is the screening of percepts. To speak plainly if somewhat inaccurately, the mind does not form concepts out of all the percepts supplied by the senses. Precisely how the mind transforms percepts into concepts is a matter of speculation. It would take us to far afield to pursue this line of investigation.

Knowledge: Justified Beliefs

When concepts are compared and evaluated one against another there results a judgment. A judgment always concerns at least two concepts. Sometimes concepts are elaborately related to many other concepts. They bring together many judgments into some kind of integrated whole that is resident within a person in such a way the person is called knowledgeable or a knowing person.

In this more complex connotation knowledge is a body of justified beliefs. Occasionally we speak of a body of knowledge as constituting a professional field. What we actually mean is that there exists somewhere a collection of beliefs accepted as justified in various areas of human investigation. It may seem strange to talk about knowledge in terms of beliefs. Customarily we contrast certain knowledge with belief states. But this is true only for those who believe in a "foundations" theory of knowledge.

This central point of many foundational epistemological theories is that sense data constitute the irreducible foundation upon which the entire structure of certain human knowledge is established. Therein lies a tale in which two philosophers play central roles. The first, Francis Bacon (1562–1626) argued that knowledge arose out of systematic empirical observation. Loren Eiseley correctly observed that Bacon's emphasis on induction need not be regarded as original with him since induction was known to the ancient world.[3] What Bacon achieved, however, was a substantive change in the way scholars viewed the world. Nature needed to be explored not in terms of what ancient authorities said about it, but through the methods of direct observation.

The second key player was Rene Descartes (1596–1650), a philosopher of even greater impact on modern thought than Bacon. During Descartes' lifetime the stock of conventional knowledge of the world was profoundly shaken in a number of ways. Explorers and adventurers shattered assumptions about geography through their discoveries. Books were being published in prodigious numbers thereby disseminating ideas that challenged long-held beliefs. Philosophical and theological sciences were in decay; the work of the Schoolmen of the twelfth and thirteenth centuries were merely quoted and not advanced. Religious revolutions and reformations, and wars occasioned by these changes, touched the lives of millions. The Copernican revolution was taking place; the heliocentric cosmological theory displaced the Ptolemaic system. In sum, a great intellectual insecurity had overtaken Western civilization. It was in this setting the Descartes began his quest for certainty and for a philosophical system that would bring pure and objective truth through an absolutely infallible method. Descartes' most important work, in fact, was entitled *Discourse on Method.*[4]

Descartes recognized that sense data constituted too shaky a foundation upon which to establish a philosophy. He discovered a foundation, however, in the operation of his own mind. "I think, therefore I am." For the better part of the next three centuries philosophers would attempt to map out the exact operations of mind. Epistemology came to be the most prestigious area of philosophical research. Most epistemologists eventually despaired of arriving at conclusive descriptions of how the mind works in the latter nineteenth century and turned the task over to psychology.

The Enlightenment of the seventeenth–eighteenth centuries cannot be understood without taking into account two principal motivations: 1) The dedication to direct observation and inductive reasoning, and 2) the passion for pure, objective, and indisputably certain knowledge. This is the reason the philosophers of the eighteenth century vigorously condemned the past. The past was filled with ignorance, illusion, super-stition, and brutality. The past was worthwhile only insofar as it was a target of "critical" thinking, a kind of thinking that continuously and vehemently attacked tradition in the name of securing a clinically pure and objective knowledge untainted by bias, prejudice, or the subjective dispositions of the thinker.

The physical sciences, especially after Descartes, attempted to pursue pure and objective knowledge well into the twentieth century, that is, to the time the thinking of quantum physicists began to enter the common intellectual domain.[5] The noted British philosopher Michael Oakeshott wrote that according to the mainstream philosophy of science the enter-prise of the scientist was "understood to be the achievement of a purely 'objective' account from which a personal judgments and preferences and moral valuations have been rigorously excluded."[6] The scientist must work, according to conventional wisdom, with perfect detachment sepa-rating pure observation from mere speculation. In no way are scientific results to be conditioned by prior assumptions or paradigmatic thinking. Unaffected by anything save objective observations and following a strict method, the scientific mind achieves a view of the world as it really is. Taken together mind and sense information constitute the foundation of human knowledge.

John Pollock noted that until recent times the most popular epistemo-logical theories were foundations theories. Someone advancing a founda-tions theory would say, for example, that what is given in any act of knowing is sense data or perception. Perceptual data constitute the cer-tain substantial ground on which the entire edifice of knowledge is built. The foundationalist states that "our senses provide us with what are. . . identified as epistemologically basic beliefs. We arrive at other beliefs by reasoning (construed broadly). Reasoning, it seems, can only justify us in holding a belief if we are already justified in holding the beliefs from which we reason, so reasoning cannot provide an ultimate source of jus-tification."[7] What comes to us by way of perception, according to founda-tionalist theories, are beliefs that are self-justifying.

We have come to believe that some knowledge is unquestionable. Sci-entific knowledge, for example, is taken as the quivalent of pure knowl-edge and has nothing to do with belief. An argument can be made, of course, that information provided by the senses is often faulty either by reason of imperfect sensory ability, e.g., color blindness, the conditions under which an object is perceived, or the expectations of the perceiver. I am certain I am presently operating a word processor but my "certainty" is based ultimately on my belief that my neurological appara-tus is functioning adequately. There have been individuals whose sense of the world was radically compromised and whose sense of self was substantially distorted as a consequence of neurological damage. The case histories described by Olvier Sacks, a practicing neurologist, underscore the claim that there is no purely "objective" knowledge requiring no belief or trust in the sensory/neurological apparatus.[8]

Scientific knowledge itself, as Thomas Kuhn has argued,[9] is socially constructed and contingent upon shifting paradigms. There is not the slightest reason, writes Kurt Hubner, "to postulate an absolute truth we are continually approaching. . . Nor is it the case that the same objects are constantly being dealt with in the advancing course of research in an increasingly more adequate manner."[10] Hubner claims that new horizons come into view which offer the scientist new and different vistas and experiences. He suggests we should give up the idea of scientists painting a portrait of reality in which details are progressively filled in, a portrait that will ultimately present a final and conclusive picture of reality.[11] All knowledge, including what we claim as scientific knowledge, presupposes a knower whose subjectivity, personal horizon, and theoretical assumptions affect the processes and results of scientific inquiry.

At the subatomic level of analysis reality does not at all appear as it does at the level of sense perception. The physicist Edwin Schrodinger stated: "As our mental eye penetrates smaller distances and shorter and shorter time, we find nature behaving so entirely differently from what we observe in visible and palpable bodies of our surroundings that no model shaped after our large-scale experiences can ever be 'true.'"[12] My senses tell me that my desk is a solid body; quantum physics tells me that my desk is composed of atoms whose nuclei are surrounded by numerous subatomic particles. My senses call into question the speculations of theoretical physicists but their arguments are persuasive. The dilemma is solved only by believing my senses as I negotiate my way through the workaday world and by believing the arguments of physics when I contemplate the physical nature of the world. In either case, however, my "certain" knowledge is founded ultimately on belief.

Knowledge, then, can be interpreted to mean a body of justified beliefs (under the rule that justification can never be absolute) as opposed to mere opinions which are unjustified beliefs. What is at issue here is not a simple dichotomy between justified and unjustified beliefs. There are gradations of justification depending on the kinds of knowledge involved and the relative proof requirements of different individuals. Further, I propose the antifoundationalist theory that there are no self-justifying basic beliefs; there is no absolute and secure foundation upon which the edifice of knowledge is built. Some beliefs, however, are relatively easy to justify on the basis of sensory evidence and the authentication of this evidence by others in the social milieu. In the area of color perception I believe the testimony of my ophthalmologist and reject the testimony of my eyes because he has demonstrated to me that I confuse certain colors. In this case the testimony of my ophthalmologist is more convincing than what I see. In any situation relating to my identification of specific colors my knowledge of these colors is justified by my trust in the ophthalmologist and not by my trust in my eyes.

Justified beliefs are in part the consequence of thinking, of comparing concepts and making judgments. Learning is defined as the appropriation of what has been thought. When someone learns something it is appropriated and becomes at-one with the learner in a more or less enduring way. As a result of thinking about concepts abstracted from percepts, a person is presented with "products" of the thought process. The individual assesses these "products" or interpretations in the light of what has been previously learned. If the results of thinking on any given occasion are not compatible with what has been previously learned, the person begins reevaluating what has been previously learned and/or the interpretations or "products" currently available for appropriation. Once appropriated these interpretations become a part of the learner. That is, the "products" of reflection are internalized by the learner.

Someone described as being experienced is a knowledgeable or knowing person. Aristotle described appropriated knowledge in reference to the framework of the intellectual virtues. Scientific knowledge (EPISTEME) is knowledge that is demonstrable as true and teachable. It proceeds either by induction or deduction. (The position I have taken, as implied above, is that scientific knowledge comprises strongly justified beliefs). Technical knowledge/skill (*techne*) is an artful kind of knowledge concerned with bringing something into being, it is a kind of "know how" that is practiced by a technician. Prudence or practical knowledge (*phronesis*) marks the individual who is able to deliberate rightly what is good and advantageous in the work-a-day world.

Intuition (*nous*) is the kind of knowledge that is able to grasp first principles. Thus, knowledge of the principle of contradiction—"It is not possible for something to be and not be simultaneously"—comes by way of intuition. Finally, wisdom (SOPHIA) is the most finished form of knowledge. Wisdom is science and intuition joined together in search for the important things in life. A person can be experienced or knowledgeable, therefore, in a number of ways.[13]

Aristotle viewed these kinds of knowledge as somewhat enduring states of mind, as resources or powers within a person that could be called upon or actualized when needed. I may be able to read French or solve quadratic equations, but I need not be conscious persistently of the

French language or the procedures for solving equations. This knowledge "resides" within me in a condition of active potentiality. A virtue, in
its etymological sense, is a power that can be used but need not be used
continuously; it is something habitual. As Aristotle would say, a virtue is a
habit of the soul.

THINKING

Thinking is something that each of us does; we are familiar experientially with the process of thinking as we are familiar with nothing else.
We should be able to describe thinking in terms acceptable to all. Such,
however, is not the case. There is a wide divergence of opinion as to the
essential nature of thinking. Definitions and interpretations abound. But
the allure of the mystery of thinking keeps us in pursuit of the stuff of
which it is made. "Thought does not strike us as mysterious while we are
thinking, but only when we say, as it were retrospectively: How was that
possible? How was it possible for thought to deal with the very object
itself? We feel as if by means of it we had caught reality in our net."[14] The
sense of this reflection, penned by Ludwig Wittgenstein, has perhaps
come to anyone who has thought seriously about thinking. Thinking, it
seems, is our way of capturing reality.

Two Definitional Approaches

Peter Angeles offers two definitions of thinking. First, thinking is a
mental activity using concepts. The activity is purposive in that it is
directed toward a goal or object. In this restrictive definition thinking is
regarded as an intellectual process that deals with abstractions.
The "content" of thinking includes concepts and ideas; the process is
directed formally toward an end. Pure rationality appears as central to
the definition.

The second definition is wider: "Any of the mental activities of which
we are conscious, such as reflecting, inferring, remembering, introspecting, retrospecting, doubting, willing, imagining, pondering, etc."[15]

It seems that the second definition is more appropriate since it
includes a fuller range of human mental activities. There are many
strands in the weave of thinking. The thought process enfolds feelings,
intuitions, sudden insights, images, sense impressions, memories, and a
host of other elements besides pure concepts and intellectual abstractions. Thinking is more than a systematic arrangement of concepts.
Thinking is a human activity and humans are not detached intellects.
Thinking cannot be separated existentially from the thinker. In human

beings there is a fundamental unity of knowing, feeling, willing, and doing. We can no more purge ourselves of feelings during the thought process than we can run a race without breathing. Thinking, even critical and systematic thinking, is as artful as it is scientific; it involves intuition and imagination as well as logic and method.

Behavior affects thinking. What a person does influences the way he or she thinks; what a person thinks influences the way he or she acts. One of the greatest mistakes in analyzing thinking is to imagine that thinking somehow occurs *sans* context in someone who exists in a disembodied state. There is no such thing as pure thinking removed from the conditions of the everyday life that touch its processes and outcomes. It is foolish for anyone to say "I reached this conclusion after much thought, and my feelings, personal history, and biases were completely left out of my thinking." The only thing more foolish than saying this is to believe it. The thinker, ineluctably, is in the thought as the singer is in the song.

Thinking is largely intentional. That is, choice enters into the thinking process to channel thinking in one direction or another and to structure the flow of thinking. Loosely-controlled thinking wanders and muses through the mental labyrinth and grazes over the mental landscape taking this or that path. At each step there seems to be divergent paths; each step seems to bring the thinker to another junction. Where intentionality and choice are relaxed, then byways are explored and thinking is given something like free rein. When the thinker concentrates attention, the process moves in a more direct and linear fashion toward a definite target.

Knowing and Thinking

When I attend to my own thinking processes for the purpose of phenomenological analysis I discover that percepts, concepts, judgments and beliefs are present in the course of thought. Thinking makes use of knowledge. On the other hand, when I reflect on knowing I find that percepts are linked to percepts, concepts to concepts, judgments to judgments, and beliefs run into and through each other. It is impossible for me to entertain in my imagination a single percept; I am unable to dwell on a solitary idea; I cannot hold in mind a single judgment. Percepts, concepts, judgments, and beliefs seem to be woven into one cloth. It seems that knowing and thinking may indeed be one operation seen from at least two different perspectives.

Any cycle of interpretive thinking begins with new knowledge: new percepts, concepts, and judgments. Sensate consciousness, cognitive consciousness, and the body of existing beliefs, in their dynamic interplay, feed into interpretive thinking and provide grist for thinking's mill. While the mill begins churning, however, one is hard put to differentiate the grist from the mill. This may seem a peculiar image but for all of its peculiarity it makes the point that thinking and knowing are intussusceptive. New judgments and beliefs resulting from interpretive thinking are either appropriated into the body of one's beliefs, rejected as incompatible with the existing body of beliefs, or held at abeyance for future reference.

The process of interpretive thinking, in addressing new percepts, concepts, and judgments, not only is undertaken within the framework of an existing body of beliefs but also is affected by prejudices and assumptions. Prejudices push thinking in comfortable directions; assumptions serve as the ground or "starting block" for interpretive thinking.

A summary is in order at this point. Thinking seems to be one process enfolding a number of interpenetrating subprocesses. That which is thought is inseparable from the thinker's lifestyle and patterns of behavior. The flow of thinking is directed by the thinker in a loose or close manner. Thinking that is done during brainstorming or conducting an idea inventory (loosely directed) is different from the kind of thinking that occurs during moments of intense concentration (closely directed). Also, it must be noted that thinking is always oriented toward some object or goal. The objects of thought may change often within even a brief time frame, but there are always objects or goals toward which thinking is directed. Interpretive thinking feeds on new percepts, concepts, and beliefs proposed for acceptance and proceeds within the framework of existing beliefs. Interpretive thinking is always affected by prejudices and assumptions.

Thinking as Dialogue

In Plato's work *The Sophist* thinking is presented as an internal dialogue. "Thinking and discourse are the same thing, except that what we call thinking is, precisely, the inward dialogue carried on by the mind itself without spoken sound."[16] The modern philosopher Gilbert Ryle described thinking as talking to oneself. He noted there is a certain vagueness of the concept of thinking, a vagueness that allows the concept to carry the weight of many meanings.[17]

If thinking is a dialogue the question is raised as to whether thinking requires language. The issue is much disputed, probably because it is so difficult to gain consensus on the words thinking and language. Perhaps it is more accurate to describe the inner dialogue of thinking not as identical with spoken discourse but as closely analogous to spoken discourse.

There are moments, I suppose, when thinking is extralinguistic and not dependent on words or language, moments when thinking is largely a tendency or orientation toward different objects of thought or thought paths. These objects and potential thought paths are quickly assessed as to their relative worth for advancing toward a more general goal. In any event, the issue is not cardinal in the present context. It suffices to observe here that a close, even intimate, association exists between thinking and language.

Thinking is more often than not a group discussion instead of a dialogue between two persons. Imagine that each person is so constituted that he or she "contains" a variety of ego states. Imagine that each ego state is the result of having experienced a benchmark event in one's personal history. All of these ego states, or perhaps only some of these *personae* are invited on occasion to participate in a conversation about various matters. This conversation is what we call thinking.

The thought exercise presented in the previous paragraph is not far-fetched. In his delightful essay "The Selves" Lewis Thomas avers that the psychiatric problem of multiple personalities is problematic because of the disordered ways in which different personalities appear. It is the simultaneity of the appearance of different selves "that is the real problem, and I should think psychiatry would do better by simply persuading them to queue up and wait their turn, as happens in the normal rest of us."[18]

If it is troublesome to imagine seriously a number of different ego states showing for a discussion that is called thinking, the same idea may be expressed more abstractly if less imaginatively: Thinking involves the recall, sorting, and application of past experiences to the circumstances present to consciousness.

If it is granted that thinking is a kind of inner dialogue, what kinds of discussion take place? One philosopher would answer that two kinds of reflective discourse occur.

Meditative and Deliberative Thinking

Aristotle maintained there are two kinds of thinking: meditative or contemplative thinking and deliberative or calculative thinking. Meditative thinking has as its content the concerns of theoretical speculation or pure research. Deliberative thinking is the kind of thinking that leads to a decision, a judgment, or act of choice.[19] Meditative thinking, however, is deliberative in the sense that at each turn in the thinking process the thinker must determine to take this or that avenue in the exploration of some theory. Meditative thinking, though, does not necessarily solve practical problems; it is not directly ordinated to a decision that needs to be made at the end of the thought process.

In last result meditative thinking contributes to and enhances deliberative thinking in that theories are generally instantiated in some kind of practice. That is, the inner discussion sometimes adjourns without reaching a consensus decision on the issue under consideration. Eventually, however, the discussion may be preparatory for deliberative thinking or may find some application to the world of practical affairs. All thinking, I propose, ultimately comes to bear on the decision-making activities of the thinker in one way or another.

Modes of Inference

Inferential thinking may also be contrasted with deliberative thinking. Inferential thinking ideally leads to conclusions; deliberative thinking results in decisions. Inferential thinking may be of three modes: the inductive mode, the deductive mode, or the abductive mode. Inductive thinking proceeds from the observation of particular instances to the formulation of general propositions. Deductive thinking proceeds from a general truth to a particular instance of the truth. Abductive thinking, according to C. S. Peirce, is "the first starting of an hypothesis and the entertaining of it, whether as a simple interrogation or with any degree of confidence. . . "[20] In short, abductive thinking is the formulation of a hunch and the playing out of the hunch for purposes of verification. The hunch is not at all randomly formulated but quite often arises out of a person's familiarity with a specific area of study.

While logical distinctions can be made among the three inferential modes, there is a blending of their functions in the real order. Take the familiar example of deductive thinking in the following syllogism: "All human beings are mortal; I am a human being; I am mortal" was probably established in the distant past after people accounted inductively for the universality of human death. The conclusion of inductive reasoning became the starting point for a train of deductive thinking. Abductive inference, most likely, served originally as the fundamental surmise that prompted the investigation into the phenomenon of death.

SOME ENABLING FUNCTIONS OF THINKING

Thinking accomplishes many diverse ends. In his phenomenological analysis of thinking Heidegger noted several meanings of thinking. Thinking can mean to contrive, to plan to have something in view of the mind's eye, to aim at something, to intend, to remember, or to reflect on a situation or event.[21] Some of the more salient functions that may be attributed to thinking are evaluating, planning and problem solving, discovering, explicating meaning, creating meaning, transcending time. In practice these functions merge and become co-actions; they are distinguished for purposes of logical analysis only. The following inventory of functions is not exhaustive.

The Evaluative Function

Thinking enables the evaluation of sense data and points out perceptual error. I greet someone who I take, at first glance, to be a friend only to discern upon reflection that I have been mistaken. Thinking screens perceptions and enables judgments about what we seem to see, to hear, to taste, and so forth. Thinking also enables the evaluation of ideas, propositions, opinions, beliefs, and theories.

Thinking enables the evaluation of previous experiences. We call forth ideas, images, and judgments of the past for reassessment and, perhaps, for revision. Previous or future courses of action, both technical and ethical, are weighed in balance against norms that have been created through reflection on experience. Metaevaluation is also possible because of thinking's ability to turn back on itself, i.e., we can think evaluatively about our thinking.

The Algorithmic Function

An algorithm is a rule of procedure for solving a problem in mathematics. In the general sense of the term an algorithm is any kind of formula or plan for solving a problem. Thinking enables the solution of problems through the invention of procedural models. Whenever we gather data about a problem situation and design strategies for attacking the problem we are engaged essentially in the creation of an algorithm. This function also makes possible the analysis of relationships and the detection of patterns.

Frequently thinking is taken as the equivalent of problem solving. This judgment is not exact. All problem solving involves thinking but not all thinking is problem solving. "Thinking is assumed to emerge from other simpler cognitive processes," states Frank George, "and from problem solving and language in particular."[22] That is, thinking is viewed from the standpoint of an evolutionary paradigm as a higher order capacity, something more complex and more variegated than problem solving.

The Explicative Function

Whatever is implicit lies hidden from the view of the mind's eye. That which is explicit, whether in the order of ideas or things, extrudes itself in such a way as to disclose some of its reality. Every event or situation, for example, reveals something while also concealing something. There are hidden dimensions to experienced reality, hidden meanings attached to speech, hidden facets of a situation. The explicative function of thinking enables the thinker to "get beneath" what is obvious, to see with insight to the depths of things, to pull away what is readily apparent and to disclose values or significances not discerned at first glance.

This function, of course, is at the heart of interpretation. It is also something we do more often than we realize. We engage in explicative analysis in social relationships, in the reading of texts, in the appreciation of a work of art, and in a thousand other situations in daily life. The research scientist who amasses experimental data attempts to tease out its hidden meanings through the application of various technical and statistical techniques. How we go about explicating hidden meanings varies from case to case, but explicative thinking is quite common.

The Heuristic Function

The heuristic function of thinking is closely related to the explicative function. The difference is this: explicative thinking pulls meaning out of what is present-in-mind; heuristic thinking searches for meaning in what is not present-in-mind. Heuristic thinking enables the discovery of new experiences and the new meanings contained therein; explicative thinking enables the discovery of new meanings in old experiences.

The heuristic function also seems to create a striving in the thinker to get at "the truth of things." The driving force behind heuristic thinking seems to be the fundamental wonder we entertain in the fact of an immensely mysterious world. Influenced by wonder, or by curiosity, heuristic thinking begins to search out undiscovered meanings.

The Creative Function

Creative thinking permits us to take various past experiences and link them in new combinations. The objective of creative thinking is the fashioning of the "new." The inventiveness that is the principal characteristic of creative thinking is ordinarily initiated by insight, intuition, and a fundamental human need to transcend what is usual. Creative thinking takes as its objects not solely the modification of material reality but also deals in the rearrangement of ideas, values, images and what is pleasing to the aesthetic sense.

Even in the most systematic of theories or rigorous of philosophies there is an element of artistry due to thinking's creative function. This may not always be obvious and it may take some explicative thinking to pull out the artistic meanings in, say, a mathematical or scientific theory, but creative thinking has been at work wherever novelty, proportion, ingenuity, or insight is evidenced.

Thinking always aims at creating meaning whether it focuses on external events or internal ideas and images. Thinking tends to the establishment of order, intelligibility, and regularity. Even while thinking is under the direction of the narrative imagination, even when thinking is creating a fanciful story of fiction, the process tends away from confusion. It is the very nature of a story, whether a narrative of an actual happening or a fictional account, to have a beginning, middle, and ending. Nature abhors a vacuum; thinking detests chaos.

The Time-Transcending Function

Thinking enables the thinker to transcend time on the level of abstract experience. We can return to the past in memory or, to express the matter in another way, retrieve the past from memory. We can travel via our imaginations to the future or to alternative futures. In the present moment we are able to profit by analyzing previous experience so as to plan for the future. This function of thinking is perhaps the most important since most of the other functions would not be possible were we not able to stand back from duration's flow to check its trends, progress, and direction. While we are fully time's prisoners we manage at least a partial escape from its embrace by means of thinking.

The transcending of time allows us to work out the relationships between means and ends in a temporal sequence, to schedule events at different points in time designed to lead to future outcomes, and to plan the periodic assessment of the degree to which a process is working toward its intended end. We can devise formulas because we think out the relationships between causes (temporal antecedents) and effects (temporal consequences). We can look to the past and uncover the meaning of single events or the entire weave of events that has led to the present moment in our lives and thereby prepare ourselves for the future.

STANDARDS OF SYSTEMATIC THINKING

One of the primary features of the thought process is that it can be distracted and interrupted. There is a positive side to this. Plato argued that the body intrudes into our inquiries to satisfy its needs thereby interfering with thinking. "If we do obtain any leisure from the body's claims and turn to some line of inquiry, the body intrudes once we get into our investigations, interrupting, disturbing, distracting, and preventing us from getting a glimpse of truth."[24] The truth, according to Plato, was to be found in the contemplation of the eternal, changeless, and pure spiritual Ideas which existed separate from the human mind. True knowledge came only to those who got rid of the body and experienced the Ideas with the eye of the soul. On its face the Platonic doctrine seems strange to us in the twentieth century. To be fair to Plato, there is usually more to his teaching than appears to the reader at first consideration.

It is annoying to be distracted from a line of thought, but this is something that makes thinking to be precisely human. Occasional distractions from a particular line of thought prevent us from becoming overly linear in our thinking; distractions open up gaps in our thinking for insights and intuitions. Simply put, thinking would not be human if the process merely emulated a computer. There would be no creative advances, no inventiveness, no explorations up and down the various paths of mind.[24]

Sometimes, though, the weaknesses and limitations of being human, intellectual and moral as well as corporeal, enter into the thinking of individuals and they reach wrong, incomplete, or wicked conclusions. Thinking becomes fallacious, uncritical, disoriented, sloppy. Thinking, to be critical and adequately discriminating, must abide by certain standards. The word critical, of course, derives from the Greek root word that means judgment or decision; the Greek root is also related to the word criterion. What follows are five general criteria for correct, systematic, or well-ordered thinking.

The Canon of Equilibrium

Well-ordered thinking is balanced in its process and conclusions. In its process thinking is critical when it relies neither too much on reason to the exclusion of affect nor too much on feeling to the exclusion of logic. In other words, all of what is means to be human—cognitive, affective, moral, spiritual, and behavioral elements—must touch the process of thinking. In the world of management the individual who is totally task oriented may get the job done but at the cost of alienating employees;

the person who is totally concerned about the feelings of employees may not complete the task on schedule. Thinking needs to account for logic, method, and system; it needs also to account for intuition, insight, and creative inspiration.

Likewise, thinking must be balanced in its outcomes. For a judge to sentence someone to twenty years of imprisonment for the theft of a loaf of bread is extreme; for a judge to sentence a serial killer to a weekend of community service is similarly absurd. Critical thinking reaches for the middle ground and avoids extremes. This is easier said than done, of course. In the two cases mentioned above there is a clear disproportion between the crimes and the punishments. In most real-life situations things are vastly more complex. Nonetheless, the process fulfills one of the canons for critical thinking.

The Canon of Logic

Logic is the science of the normative principles of reasoning, a science that deals with the rules of evidence, the process of reasoning itself, and the standards of valid inference. Logic is usually viewed in respect to its traditional and modern or symbolic forms. Reasoning, as the term is used here, is a specific kind of thinking: thinking that follows exact rules of procedure and defined methodologies.[25]

Reasoning does not exclude intuition and feeling but makes these experiences obey rules. The main purpose of the canon of logic is to ward off reliance on ungrounded impressions; logic preserves science. Reasons must be given for cognitive claims. Rational explanations are used to test refutable hypotheses. The canon of logic may seem self evident, but millions of otherwise intelligent modern adults place faith in such fantasies as astrology, palm reading, and similar superstitions redolent of ancient forms of gnosticism.

While logic is necessary for critical thinking, the danger of becoming confined by logic and method is constant. Logic is to be employed as a tool for thinking and not as a straight jacket that limits the creative movement of thought. The canon of equilibrium is to be applied as complement to the canon of logic.

The Canon of Information

Thinking always requires an object of thought. More than that, systematic thinking requires information about that thought object. It is simply not enough to present one's uninformed opinion on any given matter as the product of serious thinking. This is to say that thinking and the outcomes of thinking must be substantiated by evidence, testimony, background data, personal experience, statistics, and the like. No amount of information will insure that reasoning is formally correct and inferences are duly made, but the lack of information can also inhibit accuracy in reasoning.

If I am to make a reasonable choice between two candidates in an election, for example, I cannot claim my choice is rational if it is founded on the fact that one candidate is taller than the other. I must study the issues, the positions of the candidates on key issues, their party affiliation, and their previous records as public officials. Critical thinking is informed when it discriminates between relevant and irrelevant information, and when it orders relevant data in terms of prioritized values.

The Canon of Self-Reference

Thinking not only has an object of thought, e.g., a problem in math, but also refers to itself as it works through its tasks. Consciousness turns not only to the particular math problem but also the manner in which it is being resolved.

The canon of self-reference has two foci: 1) the actual thinking that is, or has, taken place and 2) the assumptions under which the thinking is taking place or has occurred. Thinking never begins in a vacuum. Thinking never begins except that it is grounded. Archimedes observed that if one has a big enough lever it is possible to move the world. What is also required is a fulcrum or support upon which the lever turns. It is necessary, then, to examine one's assumptions at the beginning of thinking, during thinking, and when thinking has produced a product. Sometimes our initial assumptions change during the course of reasoning about a particular issue.

Practicing frequently the process of critical self reference not only helps us "see into" our own thinking but also the thinking of others. It could almost be expressed as a law: the individual who does not closely examine and assess his or her own thinking on a continuing basis will lack ready insight into the thinking of others.

The Canon of Pragmatism

Pragmatism has many meanings. I use the word in the present context to denote the testing of thinking in practice, or the application of thinking to concrete situations. Thinking may be called critical if it leads consistently to outcomes that are productive, effective, or otherwise salutary. A person gains the reputation of being a serious thinker if he or she makes decisions that clarify ideas, resolve problems, or render things intelligible, which decisions work out in these ways in a fairly regular fashion. A critical thinker need not be infallible, but is by far more often correct than wrong.

Each of the above canons represents a different perspective on well-ordered thinking. Perhaps there are many more perspectives, but the ones mentioned briefly in the foregoing paragraphs are key to the discrimination between critical and uncritical thinking.[26]

It is likely the preceding outline leaves many questions unanswered. To linger on these questions, however, would take us too far from the task at hand. That task concerns worldview construction and not explicitly the development of a full-blown epistemological theory. A worldview has been described as an interpretive understanding. What does it mean to understand? This question is examined in the next chapter.

SUMMARY

Knowing can be construed as being intelligently sentient, as a body of what is known, a collection of relatively justified beliefs, or something that has been appropriated, learned, by a person. Thinking may be considered as an inner dialogue; sometimes this dialogue is meditative and sometimes it is deliberative. Thinking enables the reaching of conclusions as well as evaluation, problem solving, the drawing out of the implications of an idea or discovery, the creation of new ideas or things, and the transcending of time. Systematic thinking is commensurate with the canons of equilibrium, logic, information, self-reference, and pragmatism.

REFERENCES

1. Augros, Robert & Stanciu, George. *The New Story of Science.* New York: Bantam Books, 1986, p. 110.
2. Ibid., p. 130.
3. Eiseley, Loren. *The Man Who Saw Through Time.* New York: Charles Schribner's Sons, 1973, p. 35.
4. Descartes, Rene. *Discourse on Method.* Translated by L. J. Lafleur. Indianapolis: Liberal Arts Press, 1950.
5. A number of popular books explaining the implications of quantum theory have reached the market in recent years. For a good introduction see *Looking Glass Universe* by John Briggs and F. David Peat. New York: Simon & Schuster, 1984.
6. Oakeshott, Michael. "The Human Coefficient," *Encounter,* Vol. 11, 1958, p. 77.

7. Pollock, John. *Contemporary Theories of Knowledge.* Totowa, New Jersey: Rown and Littlefield, 1986, p. 26. Many celebrated philosophers take the anti-foundationalist position including Dewey, Heidegger, Wittgenstein, and Gadamer. Foundationalist epistemologists are sometimes called epistemic transcendentalists because they locate, or hope to find, a self-justifying kind of knowledge that transcends, in some sense, the human condition.

8. Sacks, Oliver. *The Man Who Mistook His Wife for a Hat.* New York: Summit Books, 1985. The case histories presented in this well-written volume illustrate the connection between mind and the neurological system. The man in the title of the book, because of a neurological disease, actually could not distinguish his wife from his hat. Other cases reported in the volume illustrate how much we take for granted in everyday life.

9. Kuhn, Thomas. *The Structure of Scientific Revolutions.* Chicago: University of Chicago Press, 1970.

10. Hubner, Kurt. *Critique of Scientific Reasons.* Translated by Paul R. Dixon and Hollis M. Dixon. Chicago: University of Chicago Press, 1985, pp. 117–18.

11. It is not contradictory to believe both the testimony of one's senses that a given object is solid and the testimony of quantum physicists who describe the object in quite different terms. It is of crucial import that we remember there are different levels of interpretive understanding. Many arguments and differences among people could be ameliorated if individuals were aware that they often speak from different levels of interpretive understanding. For a fascinating review of this notion see Douglas Hofstadter's *Gödel, Escher, Bach: An Eternal Golden Braid.* New York: Vintage Books, 1979.

12. Schrodinger, Erwin. *Science and Humanism.* Cambridge: Cambridge University Press, 1952, p. 25

13. Aristotle. *Ethics.* Translated by J. A. K. Thompson. New York: Penguin Books, 1986 reprint, p. 151.

14. Wittenstein, Ludwig. *Philosophical Investigations.* Translated by G. E. M. Anscombe. New York: Macmillan, 3rd edition, 1968, p. 127e.

15. Angeles, Peter. *Dictionary of Philosophy.* New York: Barnes and Noble Books, 1981, pp. 293–94.

16. Plato. "The Sophist." Translated by F. M. Cornford. In *The Collected Dialogues of Plato.* Edited by Edith Hamilton and Huntington Cairns. Princeton: Princeton University Press, 7th printing, 1973.

17. Ryle, Gilbert. *The Concept of Mind.* London: Hutchinson, 1949, p. 282.

18. Thomas, Lewis. *The Medusa and the Snail.* New York: Viking Press, 5th printing, 1979, p. 42.

19. Aristotle, op. cit., pp. 206–13.

20. Peirce, Charles S. *Philosophical Writings of Peirce,* New York: Dover Publications, 1955, p. 151.

21. Heidegger, Martin. *An Introduction to Metaphysics.* Translated by Ralph Manheim. New York: Anchor Books, 1961. p. 101.

22. George, Frank. *Models of Thinking.* Cambridge, Massachusetts: Schenkman Publishing Company, 1972, p. 45.

23. Plato. "The Phaedo," op. cit. Hamilton & Cairns, p. 49.

24. This is a fascinating matter about which an entire volume could be written. Thinking is precisely human because it pursues false leads, doubles back, proceeds at times by trial and error, manifests lacunae or discontinuities, seems to take command of itself and "runs away" from the thinker on occasion, and is often spontaneously creative in the gaps between one line of thought and another. Perhaps writers in the area of philosophy should never say "never," but I am inclined to believe that a computer will never be designed that improves on human thinking.

25. One of the most difficult problems in writing in the area of epistemology is selecting definite meanings for frequently used terms. If definitions are not clearly delineated, communication becomes next to impossible. On the other hand, if definitions are too severely restrictive, there is no room for expanding meanings and arriving at new insights. The reader should note that his or her frustration over the use of the words knowing, knowledge, thinking, reasoning, and understanding is outdone only by my own. Language, however, manages to convey meanings even when absolute precision is lacking. This is so because meanings are "read into" language by the listener-interpreter.

26. For a more detailed examination of critical thinking see Stephen Brookfield's *Developing Critical Thinkers.* San Francisco: Jossey-Bass, 1987. The author is at his best when discussing critical thinking. His political proselytizing in the volume is largely irrelevant. That he worships at the altar of the British Labour Party is interesting but unnecessary information. For a superb introduction to critical thinking from the standpoint of logic see Francis Dauer's *Critical Thinking: An Introduction to Reasoning.* New York: Oxford University Press, 1989.

Chapter Four

WORLDVIEW CONSTRUCTION: UNDERSTANDING

Knowing and thinking are kinds of experience. So also is understanding. Understanding is the goal toward which knowing and thinking tend. Thinking strives to impose order, intelligibility, and coherence on manifold experiences. Thinking also strives to incorporate new experiences into an existing belief structure in a meaningful way or to change an existing interpretive framework when new experiences cannot be incorporated satisfactorily into the existing framework.

This chapter begins with some preliminary remarks about the social character of understanding. Next, understanding is identified as a product of thinking. Levels of striving after understanding are discussed. After these introductory comments, understanding is explained as intuitional insight, and various structural properties of worldviews or understandings are examined.

PRELIMINARY REMARKS

The Social Dimension of Understanding

Any individual's understanding of anything is largely social in nature. When we say there is an understanding between two people we imply that they have struck a bargain or have reached an agreement of some kind. "I have an understanding with my neighbor that I will water her plants while she is away in Dubuque." I have a clear idea of what I am to do during my neighbor's absence because of the agreement. Not only does the understanding lead to action, but it also exists only because of communication between two persons.

Understandings that take place as a consequence of agreements are commonplace. After discussing an issue politicians arrive at an understanding of how they will proceed on the matter. There is a certain understanding among citizens that robbery is a crime. We have reached a

common view about someone who forcibly steals someone's posses-
sions. Historical understanding is achieved when informed persons
gather and weigh evidence, and determine what probably occurred in a
given historical context. We have understandings about what happened
in the past, what might happen in the future, and what should happen in
the present.

Out of mutual agreement we understand that certain combinations of
marks on a printed page or uttered sounds stand for particular ideas and
feelings. Language is socially constructed. Since thinking, at least in most
circumstances, involves the use of language, thinking itself possesses a
social character even when thinking is not expressed in words. In the
introduction to her critical analysis of Gadamer's philosophical hermeneutics Georgia Warnke observes that for Gadamer understanding
(*Verstehen*) "is primarily coming to an understanding (*Verstanddigung*)
with others. In confronting texts, different views and perspectives, alternative life forms and worldviews, we can put our own prejudices in play
and learn to enrich our own point of view."[1]

We are able to carry on a dialogue within ourselves because we are
able to conduct a dialogue with others. We are able to talk and listen to
our own experiences in the process of thinking because we are able to
talk with, and listen to, others. Understanding cannot be achieved in a
cultural vacuum. Human understanding is precisely human because it
involves others either explicitly or implicitly, directly or indirectly, prox-
imately or remotely. The possibility of thinking and of understanding
arises within the framework of human interaction. When understanding
occurs it is not simply an individual act, although it may so seem at times,
but involves humanity.

The theme of the social dimension of understanding and worldview
construction is taken up again in a subsequent chapter. It is necessary to
emphasize the social character of understanding here to avoid the notion
that understanding is something achieved in complete privacy, a notion
that may emerge as the discussion of understanding unfolds in this chapter due to the limitations of discursive discourse. Descriptive proposals
of how understandings are achieved frequently leave readers with the
image of a mind working in splendid isolation. This is not the case at all.

Understanding as a Product

Understanding is the outcome of a special kind of thinking, a particularly focused thinking that is both analytic and synthetic. This kind of
thinking takes new experiences apart (analytic mode) and reassembles
(synthetic mode) these experiences in such a way that they fit into an
existing worldview. Occasionally, the kind of thinking that strives for

understanding takes the existing worldview apart and reassembles the worldview to accommodate dramatically new experiences that are divergent in respect to the existing worldview.

Understanding results from a thinking process by which new experiences are referred to, and assumed into, a worldview. The thinking that strives toward understanding is a dynamic process by which an individual appropriates to self something that is "other." That which is appropriated is first deconstructed and then reorganized to make it suitable for inclusion into the worldview.

Understanding is not necessarily a durable product that inheres, so to speak, in a person's mind once it has been constructed. Unless an understanding is attended to and nurtured, it begins to fall into disrepair. Someone may understand French and be able to carry on a rudimentary conversation in the language. Years pass and the French language is not used. The consequence is that the individual's understanding of French is diminished to the point where the person can no longer converse in the language. An understanding once gained and then lost is recoverable, however, given circumstances of life that provide stimulus and nurturance.

Levels of Striving for Understanding

There are different levels of understanding in respect to the comprehensiveness and focus of thinking's striving after understanding. At the highest level the striving encompasses all of the particular understandings one has gained over a lifetime. General understanding embraces all that a person has known perceptually and conceptually, all judgments and beliefs, all that is contained in a person's memory, all skills and abilities, and the experiential residuals that remain as a result of previous experiences. At this level understanding is almost coterminous with the striving for the construction of individual identity. At any given time a normally functioning adult will have some understanding of self; at any given time the same adult will be continually striving to make sense of his or her life relative to ultimate, penultimate, and immediate personal concerns.

At lower levels of striving for understanding, the focus of thinking is less comprehensive, less inclusive. For example: I purchase a computer chip. It arrives in the mail and I strive to understand how it must be installed. To achieve this understanding I find it necessary to strive to interpret the meaning of the printed materials that have accompanied the chip. This striving for understanding occurs within my overall striving for computer literacy. My striving for computer literacy occurs within my striving for technical expertise. My striving for technical expertise occurs with my striving for personal development. All strivings for understanding take place at different levels of experience; all strivings for understanding eventually fit into the highest level of striving that, in essence, defines who I am.

Another way of saying this is that understanding occurs in reference to different life events and at different levels of experience. It is essential that we understand some things and convenient that we understand others. Some understandings are important; others are relatively unimportant. Every understanding, however, becomes a part of the one who understands.

UNDERSTANDING AS INSIGHT

Attempts have been made by numerous philosophers to understand understanding. Two twentieth century philosophers strike me as being more thorough and cogent in their analyses than most others I have studied. They are Bernard Lonergan and Ludwig Wittgenstein. Their philosophies are not similar nor do I subscribe entirely to the main currents of their respective theoretical formulations. Nonetheless, what they have written about understanding has been stimulating for my own reflection and has furnished me with some building blocks for my own construction of the meaning of understanding.

Bernard Lonergan

Lonergan defines understanding in terms of insight. I summarize and paraphrase his explanation. There are three levels of cognitional processes having to do with the achievement of insight. Direct insight refers to data and perceptual images; it results in "Eureka!" discoveries that, in turn, produce utterances. Introspective insight focuses on "questions for Intelligence" and results in formulations or propositions. Reflective insight is associated with "questions for Reflection" and produces, through reflection on evidence, judgments. Judgments that are a consequence of reflective insight come in varying degrees of complexity.[2]

Lonergan provides another key insight (understanding) into the meaning of understanding by noting that the cognitional process is cyclical and cumulative. It is cyclical "inasmuch as cognitional process advances from experience through inquiry and reflection to judgment. It is cumulative, not only in memory's store of experiences and understanding's clustering of insights, but also in the coalescence of judgments into the context named knowledge or mentality."[3] Lonergan uses the word experience in the sense of empirical or concrete experience and not in the wider sense I have proposed. According to him thinking moves cyclically in an ever repeating fashion from sense experiences to inquiry, from inquiry to reflection, and from reflection back to sense experiences. This cyclic cognitional process produces judgments which are gathered into one's knowledge base.

To use my own nomenclature, thinking strives for understanding by analyzing and synthesizing experience until insights are produced. Relationships are noted; patterns of thought and judgment are related; causes and effects are assigned, connections are made among discrete events, components of a complex reality are recognized and placed in new associations. Resulting insights become a part of the individual's worldview and serve as a basis for the analysis and synthesis of new experiences.

Lonergan's identification of different kinds of insight is important. Direct insight occurs, for example, when someone struggles with a problem involving data and perceptual images. Suppose I purchase a bicycle for a child and take it home to assemble the parts. I struggle with the explanatory diagrams and try to attach certain parts together. Eventually I have an "aha!" experience, a discovery insight that allows me to assemble the parts.

Introspective insight concerns "questions for Intelligence." In preparing for the writing of this book I read many books and conducted many interior dialogues over the nature of understanding and how to describe understanding in a manner that would make sense to readers. After years of thinking and months of writing, my own ideas about understanding became clearer as a result of a series of insights.

Reflective insight concerns "questions for Reflection." These questions focus on evidence. After uncovering and weighing evidence a person renders a judgment. Cosmologists ask what happened at the beginning of the universe, at a particular point in the "big bang" that initiated the world process. On the basis of thinking about existing evidence concerning the spread of matter in the universe, and in conjunction with thinking about certain theories in physics, insights are gained and plausible explanations are proposed.

Ludwig Wittgenstein

Wittgenstein's appreciation of the meaning of understanding is somewhat more complicated since it is stated more inexactly than Lonergan's. This is probably related to the way Wittgenstein "did" philosophy. Seemingly he worked out his philosophy through writing it out, always struggling for precision and clarity. He asked whether understanding was a state of mind, a process, or an experience. He concluded that the essential character of understanding is not to be found in any of these areas, although one may have a particular state of mind or special experience (Lonergan's direct insight?) at the point of understanding something, and one may have a series of experiences that seem united in a coherent process, but understanding is essentially an ability or power.[4]

It seems to me that the early Wittgenstein's passion for exactitude in language often got in the way of the development of his philosophy. Distinctions, the fine tuning of ideas, and the drawing out of subtle nuances in language are necessary for achieving understanding in some situations, but even these operations can be carried too far. Not only do I suggest that understanding can be likened to an insight *a la* Lonergan, but I also aver that understanding, depending on the analytic perspective one takes at any given moment, can also be likened to a state of mind or to a process. To state this in a way that does not challenge Wittgenstein's claim that understanding is a power, the power to arrive at a coherent state of mind, to experience something as intelligible, or to carry out a process involving meaning is antecedent to understanding. The power that drives the process of thinking's striving for understanding is in some ways logically distinct from understanding but in other ways implicit in any understanding that is reached.

Thinking strives for an understanding that is appropriately viewed as an insight. Thinking takes an individual thing or event and links it intelligibly to other things and events within the realm of a person's thought. Thinking connects discrete experiences into a gestalt, an integrated whole. In its striving for intelligibility thinking takes this integrated whole and frames it in terms of previous understandings. What results is intelligibility, coherence, and the ordering of experience.

Thinking links meanings. In the first chapter reference was made to the classification of meanings developed by Philip Phenix.[5] These categories are: 1) symbolics, relating to language, mathematics, and nondiscursive symbolic forms, 2) empirics, relating to physical, biological, psychological, and social sciences, 3) esthetics, relating to art and contemplative perceptions, 4) synnoetics, relating to knowledge that comes from personal experience, 5) ethics, relating to moral conduct, and 6) comprehensively integrative meanings, relating to history, philosophy, and religion. In its striving for intelligibility thinking also organizes and integrates these meanings to make them compatible and consistent with one another. When these meanings are intelligibly connected to the satisfaction of the thinker, insight or understanding occurs.

Insight and Intuition

Readers familiar with the gestalt school of educational psychology will note parallels between this school and the description of understanding as insight. Hill observes that the "emphasis on understanding, on the perception of relationships within an organized whole, is the great contribution of gestalt psychology to the interpretation of learning."[6] The question remains, however, as to the nature of insight. I suggest that the insight that is understanding is largely the result of intuition and that thinking's derivation of insight is attributable as much to art as to science.

The concept of intuition is as broad as the concepts of knowledge, thinking, and understanding. Three major connotations can be identified, however. First, intuition is sometimes understood as a belief or hunch not preceded by logic or inferential reasoning. Second, intuition is viewed as an immediate apprehension of the truth of a proposition. Third, intuition is sometimes taken to mean knowledge of something that does not entail the ability to define it precisely.[7] All three senses of intuition are no doubt valid to some extent.

Basically, however, the concept of intuition denotes a more or less spontaneous acquisition of an understanding that bypasses the ordinary manner of reaching conclusions. Intuition can be likened to an immediate understanding that arises out of accumulated knowledge and thinking. Intuition may take logic into consideration, but the intuitional prompt proceeds more likely from the esthetic sense and is rooted in the proportionality, fittingness, or quality of that which is to be understood. When a person is confronted with a new experience, the important implicit question is this: what does my sense of beauty and goodness tell me about the qualitative symmetry of this experience?

Intuition is not occult or magical. The hard-shell scientific rationalist might wish to dismiss intuition as something that cannot be easily accounted for, and therefore, something that does not really exist. Hard-shell scientific rationalists, of course, live in shriveled worlds. Intuition is a kind of recognition that arises as a precipitate of accumulated experiences. Intuitional experiences are quite common although their psychological mechanisms are not well known.

Over two thousand years ago, Plato wrote of the immediateness of intuition. After concentrated study, reflection, and discussion of a particular topic, a flash of understanding "blazes up, and the mind, as it exerts all of its powers to the limit of human capacity, is flooded with light."[8] In such an instance intuition is viewed as the outgrowth of intense striving. A person expends much mental energy in pursuit of intelligibility. When conscious effort stops, and after a period of incubation, a flash of recognition occurs in a dramatic way.

Intuitional prompts, however, need not be dramatic. Plato also noted that individuals can arrive at an understanding of a particular matter through a long acquaintance or "close companionship" with the issue.[9] What Plato meant is exemplified by contrasting the understanding of novices and experts.

According to Hubert and Stuart Dreyfus, novices pay close attention to guidelines that have been prepared by others.[10] The behavior of novices is rule bound; the novice carefully follows predetermined procedures. On the other hand, experts work almost casually and with the confidence characteristic of a master performer. The differences between the novice and the expert lies in the fact that the work, whatever it may be, has become second nature to the expert. The procedures necessary to complete the work are not extrinsic to the expert (e.g., prescriptions written out somewhere) but have become an actual part of the expert's personal makeup. The expert's effortless performance is guided largely by a flow of intuitional insights that stem from his or her accumulated experience and close companionship with the work at hand.

The novice-to-expert model is not at all restricted to manual or physical operations. The dancer, the painter, the poet, the philosopher, the medical diagnostician, and others who are expert in what they do, rely on intuitional insights or understandings that are based on the expert's closeness to subject matters or particular issues. The expert is one with what he or she knows, thinks, or does. This came to me once as I watched, and listened to, a virtuoso play a violin concerto of immense complexity. The piece was so complex I could hardly believe my eyes and ears; what was happening in my presence was quite extraordinary. Then it dawned on me: the violinist was not playing the music, the music was playing him. He was one with his understanding of what he was doing.

If the striving of thinking for understanding produces intuitional insights we call understandings, what is it that moves a person to accept insights as valid and to act upon these insights? The direct insights identified by Lonergan as "Eureka!" insights possess face validity; they are demonstrably correct at first glance. But not all insights are recognized immediately as valid. It seems that what is involved in understanding is not simply intellect, reason, and concepts. Gadamer states that understanding always remains a risk and "never leaves room for the simple application of a general knowledge of rules to the statements and texts to be understood."[11] According to him understanding is an adventure which, when successful, is a means of inner growth.

The striving for understanding is also dangerous. A person "has to concede that the hermeneutical experience has a far less degree of certainty than that attained by methods of the natural sciences."[12] Because of the possibility of error, however, the striving for understanding presents unique opportunities for the enrichment of human experience. If the achieving of understanding was simply a matter of following blueprints and set prescriptions, there would be no possibility of error and, consequently, no acclaim or sense of personal achievement when the striving after understanding proves successful. Human beings are at their best when they are somehow at risk. Because of the possibility of validating intuitional insights that are misleading we recognize we are engaged in something artful and not scientific in the positivistic sense.

We gauge intuitional prompts, I believe, not only in terms of their apprehended truth but also in terms of their goodness and beauty. In another age one could say that truth, goodness, and beauty were related manifestations of reality, and that where there is beauty or goodness so also is truth to be found. This is not to say that truth, beauty, and goodness are exact equivalents. It is to call attention, however, to the assumption that truth, beauty, and goodness march forward with linked arms. Can such a proposition receive a fair hearing today?

Whether they admit it or not, I suspect that most people validate their intuitional insights of complex matters on the basis of qualitative symmetry as well as on the basis of exact reasoning. I suspect also that those who use their hearts as well as their heads as they strive after understanding are not altogether less successful than people who rely on Critical Reason alone. Quite often the expert responds to what has been called "gut feeling" in the completion of a task and in the pursuit of understanding; the novice is usually too busy checking the rules that seem to apply to the situation. Esthetic judgment plays a far greater role in the reaching of an understanding than most of us wish to admit.

KINDS OF UNDERSTANDINGS/WORLDVIEWS

A worldview is a comprehensive interpretive understanding. Comprehensive interpretive understandings, I suggest, can be classified according to their structural properties. Worldviews can also be classified according to their contents, e.g., cynical worldview, democratic worldview, and so forth. It seems, however, that the classification of worldviews by virtue of structural properties is at once more appropriate and more revealing. What follows is a classification schema; it is not exhaustive by any means. The schema identifies various continua in terms of two descriptors. The descriptors should be considered poles of a continuum. It seldom happens in real life that worldviews can be located exactly at one or the other extreme poles of a continuum. Most worldviews fall between the poles but tend toward one pole more than to its opposite.

Explicit and Tacit Worldviews

Regarding its verbal expression a worldview—a comprehensive interpretive understanding—may be explicit or tacit. An explicit worldview is an understanding that is conveyed, at least in part, to someone else in a public way. The language used to express the worldview can be systematic and rigorously precise or mythopoeic and metaphorical. Whether prose or poetry can come closer to unveiling the truth of things cannot be discussed here in any satisfactory manner. I would not argue, however, against the power of myths and symbols as vehicles for the expression of comprehensive understandings. Some so-called primitive myths are far more insightful into the human condition than scientific and philosophical volumes in university libraries. Poets and artists can sometimes frame questions about the world, and offer hints for the pursuit of understanding, in far more impactful ways than philosophers or scientists. This is not to be taken as a denigration of philosophy and science, but an affirmation that there are other ways of expressing a worldview.

A tacit worldview is an understanding that resides within the mind and heart of the worldviewer; it is an unvoiced worldview. The worldviewer's silence may be due to reticence or to the inability of the worldviewer to translate an understanding into discursive language. Whatever the reason, the worldview is not articulated. A tacit worldview may be, and often is, expressed in action or deeds. An observer who watches a person long enough and carefully enough will be able to make some accurate determinations about the individual's worldview. Reference was made in an earlier chapter to the fact that the Hebrew term for word also means an action, an efficacious word that is done, a word that is carried out and finds itself manifested in deeds. In one sense, then, an absolutely tacit worldview would be one about which nothing is said or done.

Discerning and Myopic Worldviews

Worldviews are based on the insights of the worldviewers that constitute comprehensive understandings. Some worldviews are notable for their quality of discernment. These worldviews suggest that the worldviewer has looked at things intently, deeply, and keenly. The worldview seems to be grounded on the practice of analytic and evaluative "seeing." Important matters are distinguished from trivial concerns; the judgments and beliefs that coalesce to form a comprehensive worldview are arranged in an order of priority. Elements of the worldview are carefully nuanced; valuable distinctions are made by the worldviewer when he or she discusses complex issues.

Myopia is a condition in which visual images come to focus in front of the retina resulting in defective vision. The term is used here metaphorically to describe a worldview based on insights that are relatively superficial and grounded on hurried judgment. Important and unimportant matters are lumped together indiscriminately; the evaluative thinking that precedes the achievement of some kind of insight seems careless. Whether the structural property associated with discerning and myopic worldviews is related to lack of individual concern or some external matter over which the worldviewer has no control is not at issue. It seems, however, that the very internal structures of some worldviews cast these worldviews as tending toward discerning or myopic vision.

Provisional and Fixed Worldviews

By reason of its potential for change a comprehensive understanding is either provisional or fixed. A fixed worldview does not admit new ideas and screens out divergent ideals and values. Only experiences that corroborate the existing worldview are considered meaningful. Congruent views are always welcome; contrary views are rejected. A provisional worldview is the kind of understanding that seeks to grow, assimilate new meanings, and integrate these meanings with old meanings.

This should not suggest that a fixed worldview is fixed absolutely. One can hardly make it through life with a worldview unchanged by new experiences. The change, however, may be very slight and even hidden from the consciousness of the worldviewer. Nor is it implied that a provisional worldview changes on a daily basis or that a person's commitment to the values inherent in a provisional worldview is lacking. On the contrary, there is a kind of commitment to the acquisition of new meanings and a willingness to consider divergent views that is at the heart of some strongly held provisional worldviews. Provisional does not mean weak, faintly held, or timid; it simply implies the willingness to change in the face of experience and to learn from contradictions. To have a provisional worldview is by no means the equivalent of dillentantism or soft allegiance to principles. A provisional worldview simply does not foreclose the possibility of learning from the dissonance felt in novel situations.

Interestingly some worldviews are provisional in respect to some meanings and fixed in respect to others. Each person understands the world according to his or her idiom. While I may be willing to change a philosophical position when confronted with a well-reasoned argument, I may not be willing to change my opinion as to which baseball team deserves my support. Again, I may choose, in the light of new experience, to change my political affiliation but not my religious affiliation, or vice versa.

Inclusive and Narrow Worldviews

In relation to the scope of a worldview, a worldview may be inclusive or narrow. An inclusive worldview is an understanding that looks to all points of the compass and evaluates a diversity of meanings; a narrow worldview permits only a stare in one direction and puts blinders on the worldviewer. I hasten to add this is not an endorsement of a facile relativism. To search in all directions of the compass and to have wide interests is not the same as the affirmation of everything that is seen. An inclusive worldview embraces new ideals only when these new ideals are compatible with the existing worldview, or else the existing worldview is altered in some way to accommodate the new ideals. The characteristics of inclusivity and openness, as one might figure, are closely related.

A narrow worldview rules out certain vistas in an *a priori* manner. "I shall not read the work of any radical writer," proclaims someone with a narrow worldview, probably out of fear of a meltdown of congealed assumptions. Narrow worldviews, of course, are not necessarily limited to those who fear radical writers. Radical writers themselves may have narrow understandings of the world, understandings that seek immunity from challenge and insulation from criticism. The adherence to any philosophy, to the political right or left, does not assure against narrowness of outlook. The hardened dogmas of the left are as deadly as the cold certainties of the right.

Active and Passive Worldviews

A worldview may be passive or active from the standpoint of the worldviewer's reliance on others or self. The passive worldview accepts everything on the basis of authority. The individual who has a passive understanding of the world is always under the tutelage of someone who is perceived to have expert or legal authority; this person exerts little initiative in the pursuit of meaning and the unveiling of truth. On the other hand, an active understanding of the world never stops striving after new meanings. New experiences are sought out; there is an enthusiasm for heuristic processes. Learning is an adventure, a treasured way of life. Authority is not disrespected, but it is not held supreme as a limiting factor in the development of the worldview.

In a sense a passive worldview, i.e., a worldview that absolutizes authority at the expense of autonomous action, is a closed worldview, a fixed worldview. Likewise, an active worldview is a provisional worldview in that it is prepared to evaluate any idea or value whether it is proposed by an authority or not. The notion of autonomy itself is not absolute. No one is, or should be, an absolute law unto himself or herself, but neither should anyone be totally reliant on another for a worldview or for self-definition.

Critical and Uncritical Worldviews

By reason of its powers of discrimination a worldview may be critical or uncritical. A critical understanding of the world is based on meditative and deliberative thinking, on the use of standards in the assessment of new experiences, in the questioning and testing of new ideas, and in the recognition of what is good, true, and beautiful. An uncritical worldview is imitative and assimilates to itself ideas, values, and behaviors on an apparently random basis without attention to the strengths and weaknesses of competing cognitive claims, and more often out of whim than through deliberate scrutiny.

A critical worldview does not always spell happiness or even security for the worldviewer. Socrates is a case in point. His insistent questioning of the meaning of justice and piety uncovered the prevailing intellectual and moral lassitude of Athenian politicians thereby bringing about his condemnation and death.

Other-Disdaining and Other-Accepting Worldviews

Concerning the moral texture of worldviews, an understanding of the world can be disdainful or accepting of other worldviews. An other-disdaining worldview is full of pretension; it is smug, censorious, and conceited. It appraises the worldviews of others as naive, stupid, or malicious. The understandings of others are dismissed without an adequate hearing or on a basis of a misreading.

An other-accepting worldview, on the other hand, recognizes the complexity of things and sees some aspects of truth in all opposing worldviews. An other-accepting worldview values humility. Humility, from the Latin *humus* for dirt, is the simple realization that no individual can achieve a perfect understanding of the world of which he or she is a part. Remember, the world is like a panaoramic tapestry into which each of us is woven. We cannot step out of the tapestry to gain perspective on the entire picture. Each person's understanding of the world, therefore, is necessarily partial, fragmentary, and incomplete. The other-accepting worldview prizes the realization that all constructs for understanding the world are imperfect. Acceptance, of course, does not mean agreement. When I accept another's worldview for what it is, there is no implication that I agree with the worldview. I may, in fact, strenuously critique the other's worldview without holding it, or the worldviewer, in disdain.

Some of the continua described above are somewhat overlapping. Various structural properties seem to be correlated or attached one to another. Nonetheless, the itemization of structural properties presented here should furnish assistance for the classification of comprehensive interpretive understandings.

Cognitive, Affective, and Performative Worldviews

The previous identification of structural properties was made in relation to polar opposites on continua. The category addressed presently has three dimensions. Regarding its major orientation a worldview may be chiefly cognitive, affective, or performative. There is an experiential unity of knowing, feeling, doing, and willing in human beings despite the neat logical distinctions we sometimes make among the domains of learning. Some worldviews are largely cerebral, intellectual, and rational. Other worldviews stress affect, intuition, and imagination. Still others emphasize action, and the doing of ideas and feelings.

No doubt a balance among these orientations is desirable if the worldview is to be integral. But there is a season for everything. Perhaps an intellectual approach is the approach of choice in many situations; perhaps we should rely more frequently on feelings as a support for understanding in other situations; perhaps there comes a time when cognition and affect need to be transcended by action. In any event, all of these powers should eventually be recruited in the service of understanding at least some of the time.

SUMMARY

Understanding is described as an outcome of thinking's striving for intelligibility. There is an essential social character associated with understanding. Understanding cannot be achieved in a cultural vacuum. What constitutes understanding is insight. There are different kinds of insight according to Lonergan. Wittgenstein struggled with the notion of understanding and finally determined it is a power. Various kinds of worldviews or comprehensive interpretive understandings are described in relation to their structural properties.

REFERENCES

1. Warnke, Georgia. *Gadamer: Hermeneutics, Tradition, and Reason.* Stanford, CA: Stanford University Press, 1987, p. 4.
2. Lonergan, Bernard. *Insight: A Study of Human Understanding.* New York: Philosophical Library, 1970, pp. 274–80.

3. Ibid., p. 375.
4. Baker, G. & Hacker, P. *Wittgenstein: Understanding and Meaning.* Chicago: University of Chicago Press, 1980, pp. 597–617.
5. Phenix, P. *Realms of Meaning.* New York: McGraw-Hill, 1964, pp. 6–7.
6. Hill, Winfred. *Learning: A Survey of Psychological Interpretations.* New York: Thomas Crowell, 1977, p. 125.
7. Rorty, Richard. "Intuition." In *The Encyclopedia of Philosophy,* Vol. 4, Paul Edwards (ed.). Reprint edition. New York: Macmillan, 1972, pp. 204–5.
8. Plato. "Letters." In *The Collected Dialogues of Plato.* Translated by L. Post. E. Hamilton & H. Cairns (eds.). New York: Pantheon, 1961, p. 1591.
9. Ibid., p. 1589.
10. Dreyfus, Hubert & Dreyfus, Stuart. *Mind over Machine.* New York: Macmillan Free Press, 1986, pp. 16–51.
11. Gadamer, Hans-Georg. *Reason in the Age of Science.* Translated by F. Lawrence. Cambridge, MA: The MIT Press, 1986, p. 109–10.

Chapter Five

WORLDVIEW CONSTRUCTION: STRUCTURING CONVERSATION

"If we see knowing not as having an essence, to be described by scientists or philosophers," writes Richard Rorty, "but rather as a right, by current standards, to believe, then we are well on the way to seeing conversation as the ultimate context within which knowledge is to be understood."[1] To paraphrase: Conversation is a matrix in which worldviews gestate and grow. The provenance of any interpretive understanding of the world is communication. Understanding is gained through a fusion of individual horizons.

Conversation, whether it entails speech acts alone or other enactments of one's being-in-the-world, goes on as something natural to human beings. Indeed, it is not an exaggeration to claim that *Dasein's* inmost character results from the use of language, from communicative processes. Gabriel Marcel's dictum is apposite: To be a person is "to be with." *Esse est co-esse.* "To be 'with' involves the human person," comments Vincent Miceli, "in a self-commitment to dialogue with the animate and inanimate universe in the search for truth and to a mutual self-donation with his fellowmen for the attainment of the community of love."[2] It is not possible to be fully human in a communications void. We "become" human in a sense that transcends the merely biological when, from our earliest years, others speak to us and react to our signs and signals.

Robert Corrington, taking insights from the American philosophers C. S. Peirce and Josiah Royce, avers that interpretation—the kind of thinking that is the basis for worldview construction—is always an interpretation for others. To think is to use signs. The signs shared within a community have different meanings for different members of the community. It is in the community, however, that signs and meanings are tested, validated, and enlarged. The community of interpreters over the course of time refines, purifies, makes precise, elaborates, and translates into action the interpretations introduced by individual members. In its widest sense this community of interpreters is the human family itself. The search for truth is a collaborative venture.[3]

Persons will construct worldviews whether or not conversations are structured according to a formal model. Learning took place in the human family, after all, long before schools were invented. Just as schools were deemed helpful, and even necessary at times, to expedite learning, so also can conversations be structured and organized to maximize communication. In short, organized discussions revolving around topics selected by discussion participants can be useful for adults who wish to assess their worldviews and compare their worldviews with the interpretive understandings of others. Adults already do this, to some extent, in discussion groups sponsored by churches, synagogues, libraries, and service organizations. The question, therefore, is not whether discussions that serve worldview construction need to be originated, but whether existing programs can be enriched and extended.

PARTICIPATION TRAINING

Participation Training is an educational design that enables adults to participate effectively in small group discussions. It is a structure that organizes learning behaviors and facilitates adult learning in small groups. My first exposure to Participation Training, as an actual participant in a PT group, occurred twenty years ago. The experience brought to mind a whimsical narrative poem I first read as a seventh grader. The poem was written by the nineteenth century author John Saxe. It was titled "The Blind Men and the Elephant."[4]

Six blind men, the story goes, ventured forth to find an elephant. They wished to secure a definitive answer to the question "What is an elephant?" They eventually located an elephant and began gathering data by means of the sense of touch. The first man brushed against the broad side of the animal and concluded the elephant was "very like a wall." The second man took hold of the elephant's tusk and became convinced the elephant was "very like a spear." The squirming trunk of the elephant was grasped by the third man and he deduced the elephant was "very like a snake." The elephant is "very like a tree" exclaimed the fourth man who touched the elephant's knee. This was disputed by the fifth man who felt the elephant's ear. For him the elephant was "very like a fan." Finally, the sixth man caught hold of the elephant's tail. "I see," he said, "the elephant is very like a rope."

People have different perspectives on reality and their judgments about the world are relative to their individual points of view. This became evident experientially as I took part in my first Participation Training Institute. For the first two days members of the group were very polite and avoided discussing topics that held potential for disagreement.

As we became more trusting of one another, and as we began to achieve a continuing insight into group process, we discussed (sometimes vigorously and passionately but always within prescribed bounds) political, philosophical and religious topics.

Later I became a certified trainer and, subsequently, a member of the faculty responsible for educating certified trainers. During these years I was always impressed with the struggles of the participants. They struggled to become disciplined at conversation, to organize their thoughts, and to understand the beliefs of other group members. They also struggled, it seemed on many occasions, with their own belief systems. It appeared to me that many participants were engaged in the reinvention of their own worldviews as they listened to and questioned the worldviews of others. I concluded then, and believe now, that Participation Training, as a structure for experiential learning through discussion, offers a valuable opportunity for assisting adults in the process of worldview construction.

Origins of Participation Training

John Henschke cited Paul Bergevin and John McKinley of Indiana University as among the nine living adult educators in 1973 who made major contributions to the field of adult education in North America. Not the least of the reasons for which Bergevin and McKinley were cited was their development of Participation Training.[5] The development of this design spanned several decades.

The germinal stages of Participation Training (hereafter PT) go back to 1936. It was then that Paul Bergevin began training institutes at Anderson, Indiana, for the Container Corporation of America. A series of additional institutes were conducted in Anderson in other industrial settings. Between 1936 and 1947 Bergevin led over four hundred institutes in various sites in Anderson. In 1950 Bergevin called the program the "Training Institute for Discussion Leaders and Participants." The program was next conducted in a number of hospitals. Nurses, hospital administrators, and members of hospital boards of directors took part in the institutes during 1951–52. The design of the institute emphasized task accomplishment and lent itself well to the concerns of the workplace.

John McKinley began collaborating with Bergevin in 1952. Together they conducted the field research that led to refinements in the program. Much of this research was undertaken in the early 1950s in local churches. Also in 1952, the institute developed for use in adult religious education became known as "The Indiana Plan." Research and development activities with church groups continued until 1958.[6]

The first institute formally known as "Participation Training" was held in 1955. The year 1958 saw the publication of *Design for Adult Education in the Church.* [7] Aside from offering a number of principles of adult education, the volume suggested how PT could be adapted for a particular institutional environment. *Participation Training for Adult Education* was authored by Bergevin and McKinley in 1965.[8] During the 1960s Participation Training took on what was to become its final substantive form. Three professors at Indiana University were credited by Bergevin as making significant contributions to the PT design. They were Dwight Morris, Robert M. Smith, and George K. Gordon. John McKinley continued to write about PT and published *Group Development Through Participation Training* in 1980.[9] The explanation of PT presented in these pages is a summarization of the writings of Bergevin and McKinley cited at the end of the chapter.

Between 1955 and 1980 over eight thousand persons attended PT institutes at Indiana University. Over four hundred institutes had been conducted in the United States. Institutes had also been conducted in a number of foreign countries, principally in Canada, Denmark, Japan, and Australia. Persons from a variety of backgrounds have participated in PT institutes: hospital administrators, church members, educational counselors, military officers, postal workers, school administrators, business executives, nurses, agricultural extension agents, elementary students, and prison administrators and inmates.

According to Bergevin PT grew out of a need for adult education practice that departed radically from traditional forms of "schooling" experienced by adults when they were children. Knowles later emphasized this same motif when he introduced the notion of andragogy. A significant breakthrough in the interpretation of andragogy occurred, I suggest, with the publication of George Yonge's article describing andragogy in Heideggerian terms as a mode of being-together-with-others (*Mitsein*).[10] Andragogy and pedagogy are modes of accompaniment. Bergevin and McKinley searched for an educational design that took into account the adult status of learners, a status that required an approach on the part of the facilitator radically different from approaches fostering the traditional teacher-child relationship.

It is unfortunate that Participation Training (and graduate adult education at Indiana University for that matter) does not enjoy the institutional support it once received. No doubt the PT tradition will be retrieved at some time in the future in another place. Participation Training is too solid an educational design to be neglected for long. If it is not retrieved at its place of origin the design, no doubt, it will be discovered by enterprising scholars at other institutions of higher education.

What PT Is Not

Any discussion of Participation Training evokes in some listeners the images of sensitivity training or various other psychotherapeutic group modalities. While all education may be somewhat therapeutic, and while all therapy may be somewhat educational, PT resembles neither sensitivity training nor group therapy sessions. The game "Let's play Psychiatry" is not permitted by PT norms. Nor are participants allowed to indulge themselves emotionally at the expense of group functioning. The sensitivities of group members are respected at all times.

The PT design is not highly complicated. The design is easy to learn during a week-long institute but can also be adapted to situations requiring small segments of time. Participants can learn the design as they discuss various topics, solve problems, or work at a variety of group tasks. While many insights about PT can be gained by reading about the design, experiential learning seems to have the most positive impact on adult learners. The actual "doing" of PT reveals much more than commentaries that analyze the design. This is not to suggest that nothing can be learned by reading the books of Bergevin and McKinley; it is to state, however, that the experiential learning of the PT system is a more emphatic way of understanding what PT is.

What PT Accomplishes

Responding to the question "What does Participation training accomplish?" Bergevin and McKinley state that participants learn: 1) to plan and take part in discussions of topics they themselves have selected, 2) to see themselves as they are seen by other members of the group and how their participation influences others, 3) to help others in a group-learning situation, 4) to engage in the disciplined expression of ideas, 5) to distinguish, on the basis of experience, what helps or hinders group discussion, and 6) to establish goals, identify discussion topics, and observe group process.[11]

In most discussion groups the participants concentrate so intensely on the content of the discussion that they fall into pitfalls vis-a-vis their own behaviors and the discussion process itself. The PT experience helps learners become more aware of their own thought processes, how they are perceived by others, and the process that interpenetrates the content that is under discussion. This is done by stipulating in advance certain roles that must be taken by participants, norms that guide the group process, procedures that must be followed, and functional and dysfunctional behaviors that must be initiated or avoided.

PT: ROLES, NORMS, PROCEDURES, AND BEHAVIORS

There are four major elements of an effective group discussion. Each member of the group is a participant in the sharing and evaluation of what is stated, but there are special roles that must be filled to keep the discussion process from breaking down. Certain norms or standards must be followed; these norms must be stated at the beginning of the discussion and enforced throughout the process. Specific procedures should be followed, procedures that enable the group to function efficiently. Finally, certain behaviors further the ends of group discussion while other behaviors thwart the group in its effort to reach a determined goal.

Roles

In a PT group there is a leader, a recorder, an observer, participants, a trainer, and possibly a resource person. It is assumed the group will meet on a continuing basis. The roles of leader, recorder, and observer are filled on different occasions by different members of the group. In my experience group size should range from eight to twelve persons. Too few viewpoints are represented when there are less than eight members; too few opportunities for speaking occur when there are more than twelve members. The roles of leader, recorder, and observer can be rotated to best advantage when group size is in the eight-to-twelve range.

The leader of the group is essentially a moderator or servant of the group. The leader gets things ready in advance of the discussion, initiates the discussion, keeps the discussion linked to the experiences of the group members, helps bring out all sides of an issue, attempts to prevent domination by one or two members, and draws all participants into the discussion always respecting the right of each member to remain silent. The leader needs to guard against making speeches, dominating the group, or imposing his or her views on the group. The ideal promoted by PT is shared leadership. After a group has functioned as a team for several sessions and the leadership role is truly shared by all discussion participants, the person in the actual role of leader has little to do. Until shared leadership is more than an ideal, however, the individual fulfilling the role of leader has much to do to keep the discussion moving along smoothly.

The recorder lists key points of the discussion on easel paper and, when necessary, posts the paper on the wall with masking tape. The outline prepared by the recorder need not be lengthy. The posted notes prepared by the recorder serve as the group memory and help keep the discussion on track. The transcription and display of an outline of the group discussion furnishes the group with a visual portrayal of where the group has been, where it is, and where the discussion is leading.

The recorder makes a written account of the content of the discussion. It is not necessary to record who said what. Points of agreement should be noted, points of disagreement and conflict should be recorded, and points that remained unclear during the discussion should be written down. The recorder is free to interrupt the discussion to ask for clarification as to what to write on the easel. At the conclusion of the discussion session the recorder reviews in a brief fashion what has transpired. Ordinarily the recorder stands at the easel. When the recorder wishes to participate in the discussion, the individual takes a chair. This usually calls attention to the fact the recorder wishes to say something.

The recorder's focus of attention is on the content of the discussion. The observer looks only to group process. The observer does not actually participate in the discussion but sits away from the group to be able to scan what happens. The role of observer is often initially misunderstood by group members. It seems wasteful to have a group member "sit in the corner" and not share his or her ideas with the group. The role of the observer is extremely important, however. If the medium is the message, the product of a group discussion, to a great extent, is the process. The twists and turns of any discussion, its directionality, as well as the substance of the discussion are profoundly affected by the group process. Group process needs to be monitored on an ongoing basis.

It is also important that group members take turns in the role of observer. Individuals often talk about group process with little realization of its nature until they learn experientially to deal with group process. At times individuals experience a kind of awakening to the reality and significance of process as they strive to fulfill the duties of the observer role. Individuals are almost always more collaborative and more sensitive discussion participants as a result of serving in the role of observer.

Observers note the spontaneity or lack of expression, whether participation in a discussion session was balanced, the character of the emotional climate, whether participants helped one another, the quality of listening, behaviors that moved the discussion forward, behaviors that impeded the progress of the discussion, and the degree to which the prescribed norms (see below) were followed. Two rules guide the observer's postsession report: 1) individual group members are not cited by name for a given behavior and 2) what is reported are the observations of what happened and not the observer's diagnosis as to why something happened.

The roles of leader, recorder, and observer are classified as leadership roles. In another sense the role of participant could be viewed as a leadership role since the ideal of shared leadership, as noted above, is promoted in the PT design. Group participants prepare for the discussion, help select a topic or issue for discussion, share their ideas and experiences, help others take part in the discussion, help others communicate by offering clarifying statements, keep the discussion away from unproductive tangents, resolve conflicts that may arise, help the recorder transcribe the flow of discussion when the recorder asks for help, and take an active part in the postsession critique after the observer's report.

The resource person is someone who has special expertise about a particular topic. The resource person provides requested information and does not tell participants what to think, believe, or feel. Resource persons are infrequently used. Occasions may arise, however, when a resource person is needed. Resource persons must be utilized with great care. A particularly dynamic content expert can dominate the entire discussion. I have witnessed situations wherein group discussions have turned into question and answer sessions with the resource person directing the participants as to what they should think. This turn of events, of course, is contrary to the entire purpose of PT.

The trainer or facilitator more often than not reserves comments for the postsession critique that follows the observer's report. What is critiqued, of course, is the group process. Process cannot always be separated neatly from discussion content, but the trainer or facilitator attempts to do this. The trainer is an impartial helper who trusts adults to set their own agendas, define their own life situations, and plan the course of their conversations. The trainer generally offers technical advice about the PT design and group process. Trainer interventions during the course of the discussions are seldom made. The rule of thumb is this: the trainer should intervene in a discussion only to enforce the prescribed norms, to save a participant from ego damage, or when the entire process seems to be breaking down. Some beginning trainers find it difficult to remain silent for long periods. They tend to think they must jump up and contribute advice at the slightest faltering of the discussion process. If there is any doubt at all whether a training intervention is required, it usually is not.

Norms

Every group has its distinctive culture or ethos. In PT the development of this culture is guided by means of the stipulation of five specific norms. If individuals do not wish to contract with one another, and with the trainer, to abide by these norms, they obviously cannot become members of the PT group. Assent to PT norms is usually only notional at the beginning of group formation. That is, members agree to the norms at the level of concept or abstraction. Assent becomes real when group members learn experientially what each of the governing standards entails.

1. Shared Planning

When people come together in groups there is a danger that strong personalities will emerge as dominative forces in the group. When this happens others tend to be "shut out" of the group in various ways. As a result those who are "shut out" tend: 1) to exhibit dysfunctional behaviors, 2) to experience a diminishment of loyalty to the group, 3) to lose enthusiasm for the discussion, and 4) to lessen their participation in the discussion with the effect that many ideas and insights are lost to the group. The first norm, then, states that all of the participants must share in the planning of the discussion.

This means that the discussion topics are selected on a consensus basis by all members. It also means that each member of the group agrees to pursue discussion of a particular issue even if the topic is not totally interesting to each person. For someone to join in a consensual decision implies that the individual will contribute actively to the discussion and will not attempt to sabotage the group process either overtly or covertly.

The manner in which the discussion will proceed likewise involves all participants. The agenda established for discussion is determined by individuals in the group working with one another. Discussion topics are not prescribed. Neither are any assumptions made about the participants, e.g., that they need to familiarize themselves with various readings or that they have suffered oppression. That is, the ideologies of the Right or Left are not advanced by the trainer.

2. Shared Appraisal

The second norm states that all group members are responsible for the appraisal of group performance. While the process observer provides information about what has been observed, and while the trainer suggests ways of improving the communication flow within the group, all participants are urged to be sensitive to what happens in the group and to share their judgments about group performance. The purpose of the PT design is to help learners collaborate in the exploration of issues that are important to group members. Each group member is expected to evaluate the extent to which this purpose is realized.

It may happen that individuals will disagree in their evaluations of the group process or in reference to the productivity of the group. In some instances these disagreements may reflect different perspectives on the group, different expectations of what should be happening, or different interpretations of group functioning. If the disagreements seem to be serious, the trainer may suggest that the evaluation of the group's progress become a formal topic of discussion at the next session. Note well, the trainer does not assign discussion topics.

3. Effective Listening

One of the most obvious problems with discussion groups is that many members are fully inclined to speak but few possess the discipline to listen actively and effectively. The third PT norm states that effective listening is expected of all participants. The statement of the norm at the beginning of the discussion session serves to heighten members' awareness of the need to listen. Whether listening has been effective is something that requires appraisal during the critique following the observer's report.

Effective listening involves the effective recognition of the presence of others. Occasionally I have used a small plastic ball to help group members recognize the presence of one another. As trainer I institute a temporary procedural rule: anyone who speaks must hold the ball. If someone wishes to speak, that individual must signal that he or she wants possession of the ball. This can be very frustrating for group members who are accustomed to interrupting and ignoring others. Eventually, however, the exercise proves fruitful. The pace of discussion is moderated and the lesson that others deserve our full attention when they are speaking is learned.

4. Voluntary Participation

The PT design is such that individual group members find protection from possible embarrassment or hurt feelings. An individual participant is never "put on the spot" and virtually forced to speak. Participants enjoy the freedom to speak or remain silent. The norm states that participation must be free and voluntary. A subtle tension is created with this norm in force simultaneously with the norms that call for shared planning, shared appraisal, and the expectation that participation will be balanced among the group members.

A dilemma becomes apparent when an individual keeps his or her silence to the point where it becomes a distraction for other group members. The participating members of the group become uncomfortable when an individual remains silent. Everyone recognizes that balanced participation is the ideal, yet no one is to be compelled to speak. The dilemma usually is resolved when group members mention they are uncomfortable due to a lack of balanced participation in the group. The silent member ordinarily responds to this situation with a reason for the silence, or by deciding to participate fully in the discussion. Some persons, it must be remembered, enjoy participating through active listening more than others. Under no circumstances should the retiring or reticent group member be forced to speak. The norm that guarantees free and voluntary participation creates a zone of safety for each individual in the group.

5. Mutual Acceptance

The norm of mutual acceptance does not mean that each person must agree with whatever is said by other group members. It does not even mean that all group members like one another. The norm simply asks members of the discussion group to affirm one another as persons, i.e., to show signs of respect, courtesy, tolerance for the viewpoints of others, and a certain carefulness in dealing with controverted issues. This carefulness has more to do with a sensitivity to the feelings of others than anything else. While I may not care for the ideas expressed by someone, nonetheless I go out of my way to be pleasant and agreeable to the individual. The point of this norm is to establish a climate where comity reigns and where people can converse freely without fear of verbal abuse. The discussion group that does not observe the common rules of civility is almost always unproductive.

When the norm of personal acceptance is stated as a ground rule for discussions, group members cheerfully assent to it. Once again this assent occurs in the notional order. The norm is really held out as an ideal to be achieved, a standard that must control behavior and shape the emotional climate. In practice the norm is often difficult to internalize. Nevertheless the norm of personal acceptance is essential if any discussion is to be productive.

Behaviors

The PT design structures discussion through the predetermination of various roles and the declaration of governing norms. Further structure is added when group members are informed that certain behaviors facilitate the group process while other behaviors cause dysfunction.

A number of behaviors aim at helping the group achieve tasks:
1. initiating activities—offering new ideas, new formulations of ideas, new ways of seeing things
2. information seeking—asking for information and ideas
3. information giving—responding to requests for information
4. opinion giving—sharing opinions and tentative beliefs
5. elaborating—helping others clarify their interpretations
6. coordinating—indicating the relationships that exist among various ideas
7. summarizing—integrating various statements and ideas into a coherent whole
8. testing feasibility—testing ideas by examining their applicability to real life
9. evaluating—judging the value of ideas and expressed beliefs
10. diagnosing—attempting to discern the causes of disagreements

Another set of behaviors is held forth as facilitative for the maintenance of the group:
1. encouraging—praising good ideas, being friendly
2. gatekeeping—making it possible for another group member to participate in the discussion, inviting others to speak
3. standard setting—establishing standards by which the group can assess how it is handling issues
4. following—not challenging ideas that do not substantially conflict with one's own position
5. evaluating—measuring group performance against the norms that have been agreed upon
6. harmonizing—conciliating differences between individuals in the group
7. tension reducing—light-hearted comments that relieve tense situations

During the post-session critique the observer, participants, and the trainer should take note of the facilitative behaviors that occurred. Various dysfunctional behaviors should also be noted:
1. aggression—the expression of hostility
2. blocking—being argumentative, rejecting the ideas of others without thinking, discussing irrelevant matters
3. self-confessing—discussing highly personal concerns unrelated to the topic
4. competing—contesting with others to produce the best ideas, trying to talk more than others
5. special pleading—trying to "sell" a particular point of view, trying to win converts to one's point of view

6. clowning–disruption of the process by unnecessary joking
7. recognition seeking–calling undue attention to oneself through excessive talking, unusual behavior, or unusual silence
8. withdrawing–manifesting signs of indifference through nonparticipation in the discussion

When the observer or participants take note of dysfunctional behaviors during the postsession critique, they should not attribute any of these behaviors to members by name. That is, it is not necessary to say "The discussion was disrupted when Jim began clowning around." It suffices to observe "one of the members clowned around and this disrupted the group." This saves Jim from direct embarrassment but nonetheless gets the message across.

Procedures

The fourth kind of structure imposed on discussion by the PT design concerns the ordering of the content of the discussion. At the beginning of the discussion members select a topic for discussion, a measurable goal or goals, and prepare an outline of how the discussion might unfold.

1. Topic

The topic must be stated in a question format. Further, it must not be answerable by "yes" or "no." Field research has indicated these rules are important for the discussion that will follow. What these simple rules achieve is the structuring of inquiry and the avoidance of debate. Here is a sample topic formulation:

Topic: To what extent has our thinking been influenced by the prevailing traditions we experienced in our formative years?

The format is interrogative. The question evokes further exploration and not a mere positive or negative response. The topic centers on the experience of the group members.

2. Goal

Every discussion should have a goal so that the performance of the group can be reviewed after the discussion has been completed. The goal must be stated in such a way that it refers to discussion outcomes. Frequently groups decide that the description of group activity is actually a goal. For example: "Group members will discuss how their thinking has been influenced by the prevailing traditions they experienced in their formative years." This statement points not to an outcome of the discussion but to its process, not to some end state but to an instrumental means. The following goal statement is offered as an example of an adequate goal formulation:

> Goal: At the conclusion of the discussion each of us will be able to describe in general terms the traditions that have influenced the thinking of individual group members.

3. Outline

After the goal statement has been formulated, it is necessary to outline a strategy for reaching the goal through discussion. The following outline corresponds to the examples of topic and goal provided above.

> Outline: 1. Each person will describe the ethnic/national, political, and religious tradition of his or her family of origin.
>
> 2. Group members will have the option of asking questions of one another to clarify the previous descriptions.
>
> 3. Group members will volunteer to describe incidents and experiences in their lives that further define the traditions that influenced their thinking.
>
> 4. Group members will volunteer to describe the extent to which they currently agree or disagree with the values of the traditions of their formative years.

The outline is an advance organizer of the discussion. It is intended as an aid, but it is not carved in stone. If the group at any time wishes to change the outline to pursue an interesting tangent, this is perfectly acceptable in terms of the PT design.

Printed materials or handouts that outline the above information about roles, norms, behaviors, and procedures should be provided to group members for reference. The design, at first, seems formidable and unnecessary. Only through experience do participants gain insight into the value of the PT design.

WORLDVIEW CONVERSATIONS: ADAPTING PT

If the provenance of any interpretive understanding of the world is communication, something I noted above, adults can widen their horizons and enrich their current worldviews through the sharing of interpretations relating to ultimate, penultimate, and personal concerns. Discussions of religious, philosophical, political, social, and economic issues, as well as conversations that revolve around the issues that arise out of everyday life, can contribute to the renewal of individual worldviews, self-discovery and, eventually, to the invigoration of social values and action.

I envision the educational activity that supports worldview construction, namely the adult discussion group, as taking place in a variety of settings: churches, synagogues, libraries, community centers, service organizations, prisons, and wherever else voluntary adult education occurs. Because of the diversity of settings within which these discussions will be conducted, it would be foolish to insist that the Participation Training design should be installed in each of these environments without regard to their differences. On the contrary, the creative adult educator will assess the particular circumstances that comprise a situation with the intent of adapting any program to the exigencies of that situation. Only the very naive person will take a program "off the shelf" and attempt to use it without fitting it to circumstances. If the PT design is to be employed at all, however, some minimum requirements can be suggested.

First, in respect to roles, at the very least a rotating leadership should be established. Members of the group should take turns organizing discussions, arranging the room, and attending to the numerous details involved when adults gather for learning. Someone needs to be "in charge" if for no other reason than to direct the conversational traffic. Also, someone needs to take the leadership role in the post-session debriefing wherein participants assess group performance.

Second, the group norms stipulated in the PT design need to be reviewed in advance of the discussion. Nor would it hurt to go over these norms occasionally if the group meets on a continuing basis. These norms or guidelines offer minimum directions for effective group discussion.

Third, all group members should be apprised of the various facilitative and dysfunctional behaviors listed above. Sometimes it takes only an initial reference to these behaviors to establish the group on a proper trajectory. If problems come about because of repeated dysfunctional behaviors, a review of the handout listing these behaviors would be in order.

Finally, it serves discussion groups well to follow the procedure of identifying a specific topic for discussion at the beginning of a session. The group leader should try to keep the discussion focused on the topic. When group interest appears to drift toward a different topic during the session, the leader should mention this and ask whether the group wishes to discuss the new topic. This tactic helps ordinate the group discussion toward a definite end and helps avoid the confusion that results from undisciplined conversation.

DISCUSSING WORLDVIEWS: THE FIRST SESSION

In addition to introducing the key ideas relating to PT, the facilitator of a discussion group that attends to participant worldviews should propose the first discussion session be structured in terms of the exemplar topic, goals, and outline presented above. The topic asks the members of the group to examine how their individual thinking has been influenced by the prevailing traditions of their formative years. The goal states that each person will be able to describe the traditions that have influenced their thinking. The outline indicates that each person will: 1) describe the ethnic/national, political, and religious tradition of his or her family of origin, 2) have the option of asking clarifying questions of other group members, 3) volunteer to describe incidents and experiences in their lives that relate to the topic, and 4) volunteer to describe the extent to which they agree or disagree with the values inherent in the tradition that affected their formative years.

This approach helps accomplish at least three things. First, in describing the traditions that influenced them during their formative years, and the extent to which they currently agree with these traditions, group members introduce themselves to one another. Second, in reflecting on the traditions that shaped their orientation toward the world group members may begin to uncover some of the prejudices that guide their thinking at times and the assumptions upon which their thinking about the world and about themselves are founded. Third, group members will gain a further insight into themselves by explaining how they are rooted in specific traditions; the process of self-discovery is enhanced all the more when group members question one another about their traditions and experiences.

Group discussion is ordinated toward the development of interpretive understanding about ultimate, penultimate, and immediate personal concerns. The ideal place to begin such a discussion, I suggest, is with a discussion of the traditions that shaped members' thinking about the world and directedness toward the world. The topic, goal, and outline for the first session are proposed for adoption by the group; for the remaining sessions participants themselves should identify topics, set their own goals, and prepare their own outlines whether in a formal fashion according to PT guidelines or in an informal manner.

If members of the group do not choose to follow the recommendation of the facilitator, the facilitator should not become more insistent in proposing the topic, goal, and outline expressed above. When adults meet for the first time in an ongoing series of discussions, they are usually highly dependent on the facilitator. The facilitator, even inadvertently, can exercise powerful influences to the extent members of the group undertake a discussion of the facilitator's agenda and not their own. As I observed previously, the adult educator can easily violate ethical norms by his or her tendentiousness or lack of circumspection. This is particularly true when topics revolve around religious or political issues, or matters of personal values. Let us admit that the adult educator's worldview is not special; the place of the adult educator in any discussion process relating to worldview construction is not privileged. The insights of the adult educator are no more salutary in most areas of concern than the insights of adult learners.

There may be times when an adult educator is a content expert in, say, a particular technical area. In this case the adult educator should not refrain from "telling" technical things to adult learners. In other settings the adult educator may be asked for his or her beliefs on a particular matter. In this instance, also, the adult educator may respond by offering his or her beliefs. In the matter of worldview construction following the PT design, however, the facilitator is just that, a facilitator and not a lecturer.

Speaking from the experience of many PT institutes in which adults addressed a rich variety of issues relating to ultimate, penultimate, and immediate personal concerns, I can attest that my own worldview has changed, I think, for the better, if not substantially at least incrementally in important aspects. I can also testify that hundreds of adults have claimed benefits and personal growth from the PT experience. The PT model is not the sole educational format for explicit worldview construction. It is, however, a tested means of advancing productive adult conversation.

SUMMARY

One of the challenges facing adult educators concerns the structuring of adult conversations that lead to explicit worldview construction. Participation training, an educational approach designed by Paul Bergevin and John McKinley, is offered as a response to this challenge. Participation

Training helps adult learners organize the discussion process by identifying necessary roles, prescribing norms that govern the discussion process, pointing out behaviors that help or hinder the discussion process, and elaborating procedures for dealing with the content of discussion. Participation Training is usually adapted to specific situations. It is advised that the first session of any series of discussions revolving around worldview construction should address the traditions that have shaped group members' thinking.

REFERENCES

1. Rorty, Richard. *Philosophy and the Mirror of Nature.* Princeton: Princeton University Press, 1979, p. 389.
2. Miceli, Vincent. *Ascent to Being.* New York: Deslee Company, 1965, pp. 33–34.
3. Corrington, Robert. *The Community of Interpreters.* Macon, Georgia: Mercer University Press, 1987, pp. 10–25.
4. Saxe, John. "The Blind Men and the Elephant," *The Poetical Works of John G. Saxe.* New York: Houghton, Mifflin and Company, 1884, pp. 111–12.
5. Hensche, John. "Malcolm Knowles: His Contributions to the Theory and Practice of Adult Education." (Unpublished doctoral dissertation), Boston University, 1973.
6. The historical information about the development of Participation Training was gathered from interviews of Paul Bergevin and John McKinley in 1975.
7. Bergevin, Paul and McKinley, John. *Design for Adult Education in the Church: The Indiana Plan,* New York: Seabury Press, 1958.
8. Bergevin, Paul and McKinley, John. *Participation Training for Adult Education.* St. Louis: Bethany Press, 1965.
9. Yonge, George. "Andragogy and Pedagogy: Two Ways of Accompaniment," *Adult Education Quarterly,* Vol. 35, No. 3, 1985, pp. 160–67.
10. Op. cit. Bergevin and McKinley, *Participation Training for Adult Education,* pp. 9–10.

Chapter Six

WORLDVIEW EXAMINATION: THE USES OF SOLITUDE

Recall that worldview construction has been described as a naturally occurring process. During the course of any given day I come into contact with those whose fundamental philosophical, religious, political, economic, and ethical interpretive understandings are different from my own. I live at close quarters in the workaday world with people whose knowledge bases are different from mine. Every day I witness the behaviors of persons whose lifestyles vary across a wide spectrum. I rub shoulders with adults of different political persuasions and social classes. As long as I exist in the crucible of daily life, and as long as my being-in-the-world is being-together-with-others, and as long as *Mitsein* is implicit in *Dasein*, I cannot help but call elements of my worldview into question at least tacitly and indirectly. In this sense, then, the process of worldview examination is also a naturally occurring process.

It was suggested in a previous chapter that the process of worldview construction can be facilitated through the structuring of conversation or group discussion. Worldview examination, in an educational context, becomes somewhat more explicit and direct. The argument of this chapter is that adults generally fall under an ethical imperative to examine their worldviews in times of solitude, to reflect seriously on their prejudices, assumptions, and beliefs. The ethical imperative does not require that adults necessarily change their worldviews, but that they think meditatively and critically about their worldviews. One of the primary uses of solitude is the availability of time for the individual to examine his or her worldview.

This chapter presents the argument that worldview examination is required of adults generally by an ethical imperative. The argument is developed in some length. Next, the chapter describes areas of inquiry and investigation for worldview examination. Four general criteria for exercising judgment about elements of a worldview are explained.

WORLDVIEW EXAMINATION: AN ETHICAL IMPERATIVE

The word ethics is derived from the Greek word *ethos* which can mean custom or character. It was thought in former times that custom or tradition provided the frame of reference within which a person developed character, and also that a person of virtuous character (someone who pursued excellence) would be an individual who contributed to the commonweal or the good of the *polis,* the city-state or local community. The communal or social nature of ethics was emphasized. Recall Aristotle's comment that ethics is a kind of politics.[1] A person of high intellectual and moral character, a person skilled, prudent, and wise will make contributions to society whereas the individual who fails to develop human potential becomes a burden on society instead of an asset to the common life.

There are many ways of understanding ethics. The explanation of Maurice Mandelbaum concerning approaches to ethics deserves attention because of its insightful clarity. Mandelbaum states there are four basic approaches to ethics, none of which are mutually exclusive. The metaphysical approach seeks to discern moral standards that derive from a consideration of the ultimate nature of reality. The metaphysical approach is often associated with "a system of moral beliefs which claim divine sanction."[2] The notion of metaphysics has lost its nobler meanings in the contemporary world. Metaphysics is commonly linked with Tarot cards, superstition, New Age nonsense, and the occult. In its philosophical sense the word harbors many profound meanings. The ethical systems of Plato, Aristotle, Spinoza, Kant, and Hegel (to mention a few philosophers) have been influenced by the metaphysical approach to ethics.

The psychological approach to ethics, according to Mandelbaum, is similar to the metaphysical approach in that both attempt to ground interpretations of moral value on a general theory. The approaches, though, are quite different in other respects. The metaphysical approach attempts to arrive at standards of conduct while the psychological approach attempts to understand "moral conduct" through a study of human motivation. The question arises, of course, whether descriptive and explanatory studies can solve problems in the area of ethical theory. Is what is psychologically normal the equivalent of what is ethically right?

The sociological approach, similar to the psychological approach, strives to arrive at a solution of normative problems on the basis of a causal understanding of moral phenomena. Sociological and anthropological analyses have described variations in moral judgments at different times and places. Mandelbaum notes, however, that "variability in norms does not itself prove that all standards for conduct should be considered equally valid."[3] The correlations between social determinants and moral judgments, however, cannot be ignored.

"The phenomenological approach to ethics starts from a point which all paths must eventually cross: a direct examination of the data of men's moral consciousness."[4] The method of phenomenology is eductive in that solutions to moral problems are educed and verified on the basis of an examination of individual moral judgments. The phenomenological approach does not exclude metaphysical, psychological, or sociological considerations; the phenomenological approach does not begin with any *a priori* standards but draws upon other approaches in the analysis of moral judgments. Ethical generalizations are made on the grounds of analysis of the judgments underlying a moral act.

I subscribe generally to a phenomenological approach to the solution of ethical problems. On the basis of phenomenological analysis I formulate judgments about moral judgments, that is, metajudgments. These metajudgments are treated as interpretations. Interpretive understanding is at work no less in the field of ethics as in other fields of philosophy. The ethical norms I educe constitute, in my own mind, valid standards of human behavior in general. I do not presume, however, to adjudge the moral guilt of any person. *A moral act can be ontically disordered or evil while the perpetrator of that act may not be guilty of the evil.* A more detailed discussion of this follows below. Attention must be turned at this point, however, to the derivation of the ethical imperative that requires worldview examination.

The Responsibility for Self-Creation

One of the most frequently quoted stories from the works of Plato is the myth of Er in the *Republic.* The myth was told by Plato to teach the lesson that the virtuous person is the one who takes responsibility for his or her life. Er is presented as a brave soldier who suffered a wound in battle that knocked him unconscious. He was assumed dead and placed on the funeral pyre. After ten days on the pyre he suddenly awoke and shared with the amazed onlookers what had happened to his soul while he was in a state of suspended animation.

Er told his story. He said that his soul had traveled beyond Lethe, the river of forgetfulness, to a strange place between heaven and earth. In this meadow sat the judges who sent the just, once they had completed the cycle of births and deaths, to heaven and the unjust to the nether regions. The judges discovered that Er was not really dead and that his soul was in the place of judgment by mistake. Nonetheless they permitted Er to witness the extraordinary events in the meadow so that he could later recount his experiences to human kind.

Er saw souls arriving at the place of judgment from earth. They were weary and soiled from their journeys upon the earth. Other souls, freshly created, came from heaven and were bright and unsoiled. Eventually the souls of those who had been on earth but had not yet merited heaven, together with the new souls, were brought before the Fates. The Fates were to give the souls new lives as mortals.

Each soul was to choose a life. Some newly created souls chose to be tyrants or well-to-do persons not knowing that such lives as these were full of a particular kind of trouble. The souls who had gained experience in a previous life chose more wisely. Odysseus, for example, elected to be a common citizen so tired was he of his adventures and wanderings. When all of the souls had selected their lives, they were made to drink from the river Lethe so they would lose every memory of these mysterious events. Only Er was forbidden to drink. The judges wanted him to remember that each person is responsible for his or her life, and to report this truth to mortals.[5]

The moral of the story is that individuals are responsible for their own lives. Blaming the gods for one's misfortunes is as foolish as believing that good fortune is a sign of divine favor. Blaming one's parents, circumstances, friends, and other scapegoats is a mere waste of energy. Humans are responsible beings and what happens to them, for the most part, is the consequence of their decisions. Some decisions are sound and informed, based on experience. Other decisions are made in ignorance and out of selfish motives.

More than anything else the myth of Er brings to the fore the moral judgment that self-creation is a fundamental human obligation. Self-creation is used here, of course, not to designate the responsibility for one's being or for one's coming-into-being but instead the responsibility for shaping an identity out of what has been given at birth. The moral judgment that self-creation is a basic human duty has been constant among the wisest in all civilized societies and is a judgment characteristic of psychological well-being. If we were to select any human being as a worthy representative of the human race that person would be disqualified from the competition if he or she had never attempted to grow, to develop personal potential, or to improve intellectually, physically, and morally.

Directedness toward a state or condition transcendent to one's current state or condition is constituent of human nature at its best. It is this kind of reasoning, I believe, that lay at the heart of the thinking of the ancient Greeks when they argued that being virtuous is the equivalent of striving toward excellence in all things. Further, this striving toward excellence benefits not only the individual but also the society in which he or she lives. The social dimension of virtue is a facet of excellence that must never be ignored.

If there is an ethical norm that obliges me to exercise care in the creation of self, it follows that this same norm obliges me to take care in the construction of a worldview. This is so simply because I cannot fashion a better self without reshaping, in some way, my worldview. I cannot become a better person without changing the patterns of thinking, feeling, willing, and acting that arise out of my worldview. The issue of whether I become a better person is intimately connected to the process of worldview examination and assessment. The obligation of self-creation, in the sense of the duty of completing one's life project to the best of one's ability, is an obligation directly related to being-human. Since the completion of one's life project requires ongoing evaluation, so also does the completion of one's life project demand, on at least a periodic basis, the examination of one's worldview.

In a very real sense it is impossible to create a self conscientiously without becoming involved in the process of worldview construction. (It should be recalled at this point I am not referring to the development of an abstract philosophical system but the building of an interpretive understanding which integrates the meanings in a person's life.) The worldview I profess in word and deed is a reflection of who I am. Likewise, my ontological identity—my very being-in-the-world—finds expression in my worldview. My worldview—how I interpret and understand the world in its totality and parts—is inseparable from myself. I am an instantiation of my worldview. The interpreter is always in his or her interpretation. My interpretive understanding of the world in terms of my ultimate, penultimate, and immediate personal concerns is the determinant of my being-in-the-world.

In sum, the failure to examine one's worldview on at least a periodic basis is the equivalent of a moral failing. The mere unthinking acceptance of a worldview that has been "taken off the shelf," so to speak, can become a violation of ethical obligation, especially if such an unthinking acceptance poses an obstacle to the creation of a better self and/or has negative consequences for society.

Does this mean, therefore, that anyone who does not live up to his or her potential violates an ethical norm? Does this imply that high school drop-outs are morally culpable for terminating their schooling? Does this suggest that all persons who fail to examine their worldviews on a perodic basis are moral failures? While the moral judgment that it is necessary to examine one's worldview is valid in itself, not all who do not examine their worldviews are culpable of a violation of ethics.

Exculpatory Factors

While any human act, considered in itself by an impartial observer, may be judged by the observer to be wrong or evil, the agent who performs the act may not always be subjectively guilty. A human act *qua* act may be judged to be reprehensible but the judgment as to the moral guilt that attaches to the agent is outside the scope of human judgment. We have no God's-eye view of the world; we have no God's-eye view of human hearts, the intentions of moral agents, or the circumstances associated with the act.

This is not to say that acts deemed to be wicked must go unpunished. While we may not be able to pronounce judgment in terms of moral guilt, as a society we can, and do, establish mechanisms for the determination of legal guilt. Suppose John Doe kills a neighbor in what seems to be a backyard dispute. John is arrested, tried, and convicted of murder on the basis of available evidence. There seems to be no reasonable doubt as to his legal guilt. We cannot infer conclusively from this, however, that John Doe is morally guilty since we are not able to evaluate his intentions or all of the variable circumstances surrounding the act. There is a presumption that John is ethically as well as legally guilty, but this will always remain not more than a presumption. There are exculpatory factors that diminish or remove moral guilt. Three of these are: 1) lack of sufficient freedom on the part of the moral agent, 2) the ignorance of the moral agent, and 3) the intention of the moral agent to serve a higher good through the violation of law.

1. Lack of Freedom

Human freedom is not absolute. I am not free to jump out of a window and fly. My freedom is limited by circumstances, my heredity, the impact of previous learning, the opportunities that have been open to me, a possible hormonal imbalance, and a host of other factors. While freedom may be at the core of my being-in-the-world, the capacity for freedom is variable among individuals. What is emphasized in the myth of Er is that we must fight the temptation to see ourselves as mere puppets dangled by the strings of everyday happenings; we must oppose any system of thought that portrays human action as the simple result of environment, divine will, social circumstances, or any other agency. However limited their freedom in specific situations, human beings are essentially responsible beings.

In particular cases the moral agency of a given human being may be compromised and diminished. The lack of sufficient freedom for a truly moral act may excuse the subjective guilt of the agent but not the act itself insofar as it registers negative impact on others or on the character of the moral agent.

2. Ignorance

Moral culpability is diminished or excluded in cases wherein the moral agent's ignorance comes into play. Suppose Mary Doe comes upon a child in the street who has apparently suffered cardiac arrest. Several years ago she was certified in the techniques of cardiopulmonary resuscitation but has forgotten many of these techniques. Nonetheless she attempts to resuscitate the victim because no one else is around. The victim survives. In the process, however, the victim has sustained other injuries because of Mary's unpracticed use of CPR techniques. Mary is obviously not guilty of inflicting injury on the victim she resuscitated. Her ignorance of precise CPR techniques through forgetfulness and lack of practice is excusable. If Mary was a cardiologist, however, she may be morally guilty of injuring the patient since cardiologists are expected to know precise CPR techniques.

3. Intention

During World War II some of the German people, many of whom were very religious, attempted to assassinate Adolf Hitler. There was a law against murder in the Third Reich. In addition to this the taking of another's life has been considered evil by virtually all civilized societies. Were those who attempted to kill Hitler morally guilty? How could otherwise moral people kill someone with a clear conscience?

It would be difficult to take seriously the interpretation of any ethicist who claimed the attempted assassination of Hitler was evil. Indeed, those around Hitler who knew of the slaughter of millions in Nazi concentration camps and did nothing to remove him from power, even through assassination, were probably morally culpable. It has been recognized, at least from the time of the Greek philosophers of antiquity, that moral dilemmas exist. Sometimes it is impossible to be a good person and, at the same time, a good citizen. Sometimes, in particularly complex situations, the law must be disobeyed in order to achieve a higher good. To follow the law at all times and absolutely under all conditions does not take into account that law cannot speak to every human circumstance. To escape the threat of a deadening legalism Aristotle formulated the principle of Equity or *epiekeia*.

According to Aristotle equity is the rectification of legal justice. By its nature law is universal, but there are some things about which it is impossible to speak in universal terms. Not all cases with their special circumstances can be addressed by law. In these cases an exception to the law is taken. "So when the law states a general rule, and a case arises that is exceptional, then it is right, where the legislator owing to the generality of his language has erred in not covering the case, to correct the omission by a ruling such as the legislator himself would have given if he had been present there, and as he would have enacted if he had been aware of the circumstances."[7] The principle states that an action contrary to law is morally permissible under the assumption that the legislators would find the action not really contrary to the law if they took the circumstances of this case into consideration.

Summary: The Ethical Imperative

While all functioning adults are required by an ethical imperative to reflect seriously on their worldviews, no one must be assumed to be morally at fault for not doing so. An ethical imperative speaks, faintly or loudly, to individuals. Often this imperative directs itself to persons as a haunting feeling, an intuition, an ambiguous claim upon the attention of someone. We speak of the "voice" of conscience. Now conscience is actually an interpretive judgment based on evidence and reasoning, but this act of interpretive judgment is often preceded by an apprehension that not all is well. Conscience has no "voice" but the metaphor is apt.

It is not claimed, therefore, that all adults who do not examine their worldviews are guilty of moral failure. More likely than not the majority of those we call disadvantaged lack sufficient freedom to choose not to develop their potential to the fullest or have not reached the developmental stage that allows them to see the necessity of creating a better self. They may lack knowledge; they may act out of honestly formed intentions that are contrary to the ethical imperative. Various circumstances of a person's life can forestall the application of the ethical imperative requiring worldview examination. Thus, it is possible for someone to have an intention contrary to the ethical imperative because the person judges that the circumstances in his or her life are such as to hold the imperative in abeyance. This does not mean, of course, that the ethical imperative ceases to be. The ethical imperative comes into being for individuals only at the point in their lives wherein they become aware of their worldviews and are able to evaluate their worldviews.

Once a person recognizes the ethical imperative that requires worldview examination a question immediately comes to mind: How do I go about an examination of my worldview?

WORLDVIEW EXAMINATION PROCEDURES

What aspects of a worldview need examination on at least a periodic basis? Where should attention be focused? What are the targets of an evaluative analysis?

Adults should examine selected prejudices, assumptions, and beliefs in the realms of ultimate, penultimate, and personal concern, and should assess the degree to which their actions are consistent with these prejudices, assumptions, and beliefs.

The basis for the selection of these worldview elements and the precise identification of specific prejudices, assumptions, and beliefs must be determined by each individual. One way to approach this selection is through a reflection on current life situations that seem problematic. If I find I am having difficulties living harmoniously with my spouse and children, if I cannot make friends, or if I am at odds with people in the workplace, it would probably be helpful for me to examine prejudices, assumptions, and beliefs associated with interpersonal relationships. Again, if I begin to feel uncomfortable with any of my belief sets (religious, political, ethical, etc.), this is probably sufficient reason to undertake a study of the specific belief set. Finally, if I feel totally content with my worldview and satisfied with all of my patterns of thinking, feeling, and acting, it is perhaps necessary for me to seek to understand the prejudices, assumptions, and beliefs that ground my complacency and self-satisfaction.

The word prejudice is used here in its pre-Enlightenment, nonpejorative sense: a prejudice is a provisional judgment based on accumulated experience and is recognized as a provisional judgment that may need further study. Assumptions are similar to prejudices. Assumptions, however, are more likely to be stated in propositional terms whereas prejudices take affective expression when they are unhidden. An assumption, whether hidden or not, is usually a foundation upon which a line of reasoning is established. Inferences can always be traced to some kind of assumption that functions as a point of origination for thinking. Prejudices function as guiding structures, often hidden, that channel thinking along familiar paths. They operate in a more subtle way than assumptions.

Beliefs may be grounded or unfounded. Unfounded beliefs are opinions. Grounded beliefs may be established on the basis of sense data as in "I believe I am seated" or on the basis of inference as in "I believe the cosmos began billions of years ago with a big bang and that the universe has been expanding ever since." Beliefs are grounded in many diverse ways. A religious belief, for example, may be grounded on interpretations of past events and testimony about these interpretations that have been transmitted from one generation to another. A political belief may be grounded on the comparison of two or more political parties and the inferences that arise out of the comparison. A personal belief such as "I enjoy friendly relations with my co-workers" may be grounded on a sense of fellowship experienced in the workplace.

In summary, a prejudice is defined as an orientation toward a particular judgment; an assumption is a prejudice that has become a basis for a line of reasoning. An unfounded belief results from a line of reasoning that is flawed and lacking evidence. A grounded belief results from critical reasoning that accounts for evidence.

Prejudices, assumptions, beliefs, and actions refer to the three areas of human concern already stipulated, that is, to matters of ultimate, penultimate, and immediate personal concerns. In the area of ultimate concern prejudices, assumptions, and beliefs revolve around issues such as the ultimate origin and destiny of the world, the reality or nonreality of God, the purpose of human history, the meaning of natural evolution, and so forth. Most often these prejudices, assumptions, beliefs, and actions will revolve around religious affirmations and practice. This is not to say, of course, that the worldviews of atheists or agnostics are free of prejudices, assumptions, and beliefs that somehow need not be examined.

In the area of penultimate concern various political, social, economic, ethical, and similar issues are associated with sets of prejudices, assumptions, and beliefs. In the area of immediate personal concern the focus is on prejudices, assumptions, and beliefs that refer to life goals, life activities, and relationships.

Some examples may help clarify the matter under discussion. A prejudice in the area of ultimate concern may be someone's generalized feeling that prayer is an effective way of dealing with problems, or to the contrary, the generalized feeling of another person that prayer is a superstitious practice. Perhaps both of these affective orientations need examination; perhaps both prejudices are excessive. A prejudice in the area of penultimate concern may be a sense that a particular political party is better than another. In the area of personal concern someone may feel that he or she would enjoy a particular career.

An assumption in the area of ultimate concern could be the assumption that order postulates intelligence. This assumption then serves as the foundation for a line of reasoning that argues the order in the world postulates the reality of a divine intelligence. The assumptions that the Democratic party is the party of the little people or that the Republican party is the party fighting big government can represent starting places for thinking out one's party allegiance. Finally, the assumption that the possession of much wealth leads to contentment and happiness may be the beginning of a thought process that leads someone into a lucrative career or into crime.

A belief that the process of cosmic evolution is leading to some ineffable Point Omega or the belief that the world is some sort of immense computer working out an algorithm are examples of beliefs in the area of ultimate concern. Both of these beliefs are more than simple assumptions since they have been argued with some rigor.[7] The belief that the current trade imbalance between the United States and foreign competitors represents an economic threat to the United States is an example of a penultimate belief. My belief that a daily walk is good for me exemplifies a belief in the arena of immediate personal concern.

Prejudices, assumptions, and beliefs, as noted above, are quite similar. We can distinguish them by saying the prejudices channel thinking along familiar paths, assumptions are usually simple propositional starting points for thinking, and beliefs are more or less justified, developed, and complex positions taken on issues. In practice, however, prejudices, assumptions, and beliefs interpenetrate one another. A prejudice can strengthen an assumption or belief; a belief can be inseparable from the assumption that supports it.

No doubt there are more prejudices, assumptions, and beliefs than can be measured in many sittings. The individual who sets about to examine his or her worldview should take a blank page, delineate three columns (prejudices, assumptions, beliefs) and three rows (ultimate, penultimate, and personal concerns), and begin identifying elements for examination. There is no need to labor over the discrimination of prejudices, assumptions, and beliefs. In this procedure intuition should be trusted. Anyone who examines his or her worldview on a regular, periodic basis will soon discover the prejudices, assumptions and beliefs most in need of evaluative analysis.

The most important aspect of a worldview is its instantiation in practice, the living out of prejudices, assumptions, and beliefs. There is probably no easy way to attempt to understand the correlation between our deeds and our prejudices, assumptions, and beliefs. Most of us have an almost infinite capacity for self-delusion when it comes to the assessment of our deeds and misdeeds. It sometimes helps, though, to keep a diary that itemizes patterns of actual behavior which reflect or betray beliefs. As with so many other aspects of life, practice makes perfect. The person who examines his or her actions regularly, I believe, is more likely to live in concordance with beliefs than the individual who never assesses his or her behavior. Periodic worldview analysis will also uncover the truth about one's prejudices and assumptions.

Guidelines for Evaluative Analysis

There are four general guidelines, I suggest, for evaluating prejudices, assumptions, and beliefs. First, it is necessary to inquire about the antecedents of prejudices, assumptions, and beliefs. Second, it is necessary to project the outcomes or consequences of prejudices, assumptions, and beliefs. Third, prejudices, assumptions, and beliefs should be examined in relation to their inherent reasonableness. Finally, the worldview examiner should ask what intuition says about this particular prejudice, assumption, or belief.

1. Examining Antecedents

A worldview is obviously related to the worldviewer's previous experience. If I entertain a particular prejudice, a particular provisional judgment, it is because my experience (notably my tradition) has been a seedbed for the prejudice. To understand the prejudice I must attempt to gain a better understanding of its origination. Therefore, I recount in memory and reflection all of the experiences that have influenced me in the specific matter embraced by the prejudice.

Suppose I entertain a prejudice that favors a political party. Each election I merely pull one lever and vote the straight party ticket. In examining my behavior and the corresponding prejudice that influences behavior I come to understand the prejudice more clearly. My grandparents and parents supported the party. They often praised the party and its philosophy. My favorite uncle was a precinct captain and as a child I often went with him in his rounds of the neighborhood. My prejudice is rooted in happy memories. I ask myself whether my current position on political issues is a thoughtful one or whether I have merely taken a political philosophy "off the shelf." Once I understand the forces that have shaped my prejudice, I am ready to examine the prejudice further.

2. Examining Consequences

To reach an interpretive understanding of one's interpretive understanding of the world (a self-referencing understanding) it is necessary to look to the past in an attempt to discover the source events of prejudices, assumptions, and beliefs. To gain an even more complete understanding it is necessary to investigate the likely consequences of prejudices, assumptions, and beliefs. The forecasting of consequences is a central operation in any decision-making model; it is also a cardinal element in the examination of the prejudices, assumptions, and beliefs associated with a worldview. Given this belief or set of beliefs, this or that event will probably follow.

The interpretation of the consequences of affirming a particular belief, for example, depends largely on the ability of imaginative reasoning, the process whereby various scenarios are imagined as a result of thinking projectively. If the consequences of a belief are negative for the worldviewer, for other persons around the worldviewer, or for society itself, the belief must be examined more thoroughly before it can be validated. Unfortunately the consequences of some beliefs are both positive and negative, or positive in respect to the worldviewer and negative in respect to others. Very seldom are consequences of prejudices, assumptions, and beliefs clearly drawn.

Let us return to the example of my prejudice in favor of a political party. I have already determined its antecedents: I was influenced strongly by the political allegiances of my grandparents, parents, and favorite uncle. Now I must inquire about the consequences of my allegiance to the party and my practice of voting the straight party ticket. One consequence is that the party will remain strong in my region if it can count on loyal members such as myself. On the other hand, the practice of voting a straight party ticket may be a device that keeps me from thinking through the issues. Also, a candidate from another party may, on occasion, be more thoughtful, more insightful, more responsive, and more candid than the candidate of the party I support. Further analysis is needed.

3. Examining Reasonableness

Once a prejudice, assumption, or belief has been formulated or expressed discursively with some degree of precision, it is possible to examine the proposition in relation to its reasonableness. Sometimes all that is necessary to unmask an assumption as unreasonable is to state the assumption in unambiguous language. Reasonableness also refers to the correlation of a particular assumption with the other prejudices, assumptions, and beliefs maintained by the worldviewer. Again, the unreasonableness of an assumption occasionally becomes apparent when the worldviewer discovers the assumption is not consistent with the rest of the worldview.

The example of my prejudice in favor of the political party is again pertinent. In my examination of this prejudice I have found how it originated and I have weighed some of its consequences. Now I inquire as to the reasonableness of voting a straight party ticket. It seems that when it comes to politics I put my life on automatic pilot; the more I think about the prejudice I begin to understand it is not reasonable to vote for any candidate simply because he or she wears the tag of a political party. Also, I examine this prejudice in the light of my belief that all citizens should vote only if they have informed themselves and studied the issues carefully. It is more reasonable, I conclude, to take account also of the character of individual candidates and the positions they take on vital issues of the day. I am inclined to reject my prejudice.

4. Examining Intuition

The worldviewer, I advise, should also ask whether a specific prejudice, assumption, or belief "feels" right, whether the worldviewer is comfortable with it. Something akin to esthetic judgment comes into play in the evaluation of elements of a worldview. Esthetic judgment, taste, diagnostic insight (call it what you wish) enters into the assessments we make every day in the actual world. We are reluctant, however, to admit that important matters are decided on extra-logical grounds. Mention was made above of the metaphorical way of referring to conscience as an inner "voice." This "voice" often represents the accumulated experience of an individual who is confronted with problematic alternatives. As long as a person critiques prejudices, assumptions, and beliefs in terms of how they came to be, what their consequences might be, and their relative reasonableness, it seems highly advantageous to bring personal intuition and imagination into the evaluative analysis.

We revisit for a final time the example of my political loyalty. After examining my political prejudice in relation to its antecedents, possible consequences, and reasonableness, I am inclined to reject the prejudice and the practice of voting a straight party ticket. Still, it does not feel right for me to repudiate my long-standing commitment to the party. Certainly I could never become an active member of another party. Intuitive insight discloses to me that I can claim formal membership in my favored party while at the same time reserving my right to split the ticket in the voting booth. In other words, I can subscribe generally to the philosophy of the party but I need not vote mindlessly or on instructions from others. My prejudice, upon thorough examination, has undergone some changes. It is still present in some sense, but it has been transformed to a great extent in the light of evaluative analysis in that it is no longer a provisional judgment. Under evaluative analysis the prejudice has been brought before the tribunal of critical judgment and a grounded belief has emerged.

There are times when rationality and intuition come into conflict. Reason may tell me that voting a straight party ticket is not appropriate while intuition tells me the opposite. If I admit the inappropriateness of voting the straight party ticket, I have listened to reason and rejected intuition. I may say "Voting the straight party ticket is inappropriate" and continue to vote the straight party ticket. In this latter case I have listened to intuition after paying lip service to reason.

The foregoing example is perhaps somewhat simple as are most examples. (I have no idea, by the way, if voting the straight party ticket, in general, is praiseworthy or blameworthy.) The examination of prejudices, assumptions, and beliefs (and corresponding actions) in relation to the four general guidelines is often extremely complex and mentally arduous. Nevertheless the example indicates the manner in which the criteria can be applied.

The approach for worldview examination presented here is but a single approach out of many that would prove beneficial. Techniques are helpful tools for the conducting of any enterprise; there are no techniques, however, that are productive in every case and under all circumstances. Many worldviewers would probably do well to eschew techniques suggested by others and invent their own investigative methods. If worldviewers are mature enough and serious enough to begin an evaluative analysis of their worldviews, it is likely they are creative enough to devise their own assessment strategies and techniques. Of course, the encounter with suggested techniques often stimulates creative adults to design their own. As long as the following of suggested techniques is not mindlessly imitative, the worldviewer stands a good chance of accomplishing a sound evaluative analysis.

Something must be stated, albeit briefly, about the kind of worldview examination that occurs in the wake of traumatic events in the lives of adults. The death of a spouse, a diagnosis of a chronic illness, the loss of a job, a divorce, an injury, and similar traumatic events often trigger questions about worldviews. Sometimes dearly held beliefs, values, and modes of action come under serious questioning. Quite often the pain of the traumatic experience triggers inquiry but then gets in the way of a thorough worldview examination. The adult who is questioning his or her worldview at this point needs to move out of solitude and find someone with whom to talk. This "someone" need not be wise and full of answers; normally functioning adults do not need gurus. All that is required is someone who is willing to listen and to help sort out ideas and alternatives. The examination of a worldview within one's solitude is prescribed for most adults; worldview examination prompted by severe emotional pain needs to get out of solitude because the echoes of emotional pain in one's solitude frequently interfere with the inner dialogue we call thinking.[8]

SUMMARY

There is an ethical imperative that requires worldview examination. This imperative explicitly commands human beings to complete their life projects, to grow, to actualize their potential. This implies the development of their worldviews. Such development occurs in the push and pull of the workaday world, as a result of educational activities, and through the uses of individual solitude. One procedure for structuring the examination of worldviews includes the identification of prejudices, assumptions, and beliefs in the areas of ultimate, penultimate, and immediate personal concerns. The four general guidelines for the evaluative analysis of prejudices, assumptions, and beliefs concern: 1) an understanding of the antecedents of prejudices, assumptions, and beliefs, 2) an understanding of their consequences, 3) an understanding of their relative reasonableness, and 4) an understanding of one's own intuition in respect to specific prejudices, assumptions, and beliefs.

REFERENCES

1. Aristotle. *Ethics.* Translated by J. A. K. Thomson, New York: Penguin Books, Reprint, 1986. p. 64.
2. Mandelbaum, Maurice. *Phenomenology of Moral Experience.* Baltimore: Johns Hopkins Press, 1969, p. 16.
3. Ibid. p. 26. Relativists would claim that since there is such a wide variability of ethical norms from culture to culture there are really no universal norms delineating moral from immoral behavior. This position confuses the descriptive and normative orders. The position also fails to see norms as representing ideals that help human beings grow morally. Their fear of moral norms of universal validity is perhaps based on the mistaken view that any violation of a universal norm results in moral culpability. One may violate a universal norm,

as I explain in the chapter, and yet not be adjudged guilty of violation due to extenuating and exculpatory circumstances. The recognition of universally valid ethical norms does not mean that we must give ourselves over to stultifying legalism. I recognize that the position I have taken is likely to be called relativist. I reject the label. I believe in absolute and universal ethical imperatives, many of which can be strongly justified. The knowledge of these imperatives by any one person, however, must necessarily be relative to that individual's limited horizon. We unveil ethical truths through the fusion of horizons.

4. Ibid. p. 30.

5. Plato. "The Republic," in *Great Dialogues of Plato.* Translated by W. H. D. Rouse. New York: A Mentor Book, 13th printing, 1956, pp. 415–22.

6. Op. cit, Aristotle, p. 199.

7. Refer to *The Anthropic Cosmological Principle* by John Barrow and Frank Tipler for a tightly reasoned argument about the end of the world, Point Omega, from a point of view of theoretical physics. Barrow, an astronomer at the University of Sussex, and Tipler, mathematical physicist at Tulane University, call their approach "physical eschatology." Their conclusion, after over 600 pages of argument, is summed up in two sentences: "At the instant the Point Omega is reached, life will have gained control of all matter and forces not only in a single universe but in *all* universes whose existence is logically possible; life will have spread into *all* spatial regions in all universes which could possibly exist, and will have stored an infinite amount of information, including *all* bits of knowledge which is logically possible to know. And this is the end." Oxford: Oxford University Press, 1988, P. 667. Anent the theory that the world is a computer, see Robert Wright's *Three Scientists and Their Gods.* New York: Harper and Row, 1989, pp. 1–72.

8. There are times when it is necessary to get away from the distractions of everyday life, times when a retreat to solitude is necessary if we are to conduct a serious evaluation of our lives and worldviews. On the other hand, there are times when the company of at least one other human being is needed. In communicating with this other human being we sort out our ideas and are able to "hear" what we are thinking. The other person also provides support and encouragement; this is needed in the aftermath of traumatic experience that triggers worldview examination.

Chapter Seven

ADULT EDUCATION AND WORLDVIEW CONSTRUCTION

Adults will construct interpretive understandings of the world without educational interventions just as they can learn outside of a formal educational setting. Worldview construction takes place in the home, in the marketplace, on the playing field, and in association with others in hundreds of nonschool or nonprogram contexts. This is not to say, however, that education has not been used instrumentally to serve the purpose of worldview construction. Worldview construction may not be explicitly and formally stated as a goal of education in general, and adult education in particular, but insofar as any educational experience contributes to a person's interpretive understanding of the world, education is involved in worldview construction.

Adult education theorists have recognized the association between education and worldview construction without expressly using the words "worldview construction." Many of the goals they identify as proper to the work of adult education are related to the process of worldview construction. The ideas of several of these theorists are noted here to support this claim.

N. F. S. Grundtvig was a nineteenth century Danish philosopher-theologian-educationist-legislator whose ideas made an important impact on the thinking of Eduard Lindeman, a leading founder of American adult education.[1] Grundtvig proposed the idea of folk high school for those over eighteen years of age, a school without a rigidly fixed curriculum. The school was not to impart technical or vocational skills; cotter's schools, trade schools, agricultural schools were already established in Denmark in the 1830s for these purposes. The school was not to be subject centered but rather focused to a large extent on the interests of the learners.[2]

The purposes served by the school were: 1) the establishment of a clearer view of human and civic relationships and 2) the development of a livelier appreciation of the national fellowship from which issued everything great and good in the learner's heritage. Grundtvig was a nationalist in the sense he valued, and believed other Danes should appreciate, the heritage and tradition that grounded their existence as members of a national community. Learners were to be awakened and enlightened, and this was to be accomplished by means of the interchange of ideas via "free talk," what Grundtvig called the living word. Obviously the purposes of the school served also the process of what is described in these pages as worldview construction. Through the interchange of ideas, by means of open discussions, the adult learners were to examine their ideals and outlooks, their history and heritage.

Eduard Lindeman transported much of Grundtvig's philosophy to America. Much of this philosophy was highlighted in 1926 in *The Meaning of Adult Education,* a benchmark publication in the history of adult education in America. Education, according to Lindeman, was not a preparation for life but was coextensive with life. Adult education revolves around nonvocational ideals. ". . .adult education more accurately defined begins where vocational education leaves off. Its purpose is to put meaning into the whole of life."[3] Adult education was not to be identified with the systematic study of subjects but rather with the analysis of situations. The best resource for adult education was the experience of the learner.

Worldview construction, as described previously, concerns the putting of meaning into life. This is accomplished principally through the analysis and interpretation of life situations. This analytic and interpretive process is ongoing; personal experience is foundational for the process. It does not distort Lindeman's meaning to interpret adult education as having a supereminent goal relating to the facilitation of worldview construction.

Paul Bergevin was influenced by Grundtvig, Lindeman, and to a large extent, by Aristotle. Bergevin maintained that adult education functions to achieve purposes transcendent to whatever topic adults happen to be studying. The teacher who helps adults learn how to make chairs, for example, must also in some way help them to better themselves as human beings. Adult education has several general goals among which are: 1) helping adults achieve a degree of happiness and meaning in life, 2) helping adults understand themselves, their talents, their limitations, and their relationships with others, 3) helping adults understand the need for lifelong learning, 4) providing opportunities to help adults grow spiritually, culturally, physically, politically, and vocationally, and 5) providing education for survival, i.e., literacy education, health education, and vocational skills training.[4]

Bergevin's emphasis on the acquisition of happiness and meaning, and the attainment of understanding through adult education stands forth as central to his philosophy. These ends were to be sought, he stated, even when the content of an educational program concerned everyday, mundane, or technical matters. A transcendent goal and the possibilities of profound understanding come into being whenever adults gather in a purposeful way. He once remarked to me that the twenty minute break in his three-hour graduate seminar in adult education philosophy was the most important part of the afternoon. "Just look at them," he directed. "Real learning is taking place in so many ways."[5] Bergevin would not argue with the proposition that the facilitation of worldview construction was an important aim of adult education. I was privileged to participate in sometimes lengthy discussions with Bergevin that addressed the needs of adults to order their lives, to find coherence and meaning in life, before they could achieve anything resembling happiness.

Jerold Apps expressed some of his philosophical beliefs anent adult education after reviewing the various competing philosophies of education. Apps stated his belief that human beings were more than mere animals and that they had minds and souls. He indicated that people are constantly searching to understand themselves, their relationships with the natural and social environments, and how they relate to a Higher Being. For Apps learning is a process by which we seek these and various other understandings. [6]

Again, App's views reflect an orientation to what has been described here as worldview construction. Adults are constantly striving for understanding. They seek interpretations that bring understanding and meaning to their lives. This quest is ongoing throughout life.

More recently Stephen Brookfield envisioned adult education as involving the identification of external sources and internalized assumptions framing human conduct. He called for the critical assessment of these sources and assumptions. "Such critical awareness will involve a realization of the contextual, provisional, and relative nature of supposed 'truth,' public knowledge and personal belief." Once assumptions are perceived as irrelevant and inauthentic, there will follow a transformation of individual and collective circumstances. This transformation becomes apparent in the renegotiation of personal relationships, the bestowal of significance to the conditions of work, and an engagement in the alteration of social forms.[7]

What each of these theorists postulates as goals of adult education, speaking out of different interpretive understandings of the world, is that adult education is not simply training nor is it the transmission of subject matter. Adult education, to use my language, is and can be a major factor in helping adults construct the network of ideas, values, feelings, beliefs, opinions, intuitions, judgments, choices, and actions that constitute a worldview. Historically adult education has been recognized as a force for individual and societal growth; it has also been concerned with worldview construction, albeit these precise words have not been used by adult education theorists explicitly. I suggest there is a common vision shared by the theorists mentioned above and that this vision is directly relevant to what I have called worldview construction.

It may be objected that worldview construction has been defined so broadly as to include almost any philosophical statement of the ideal goals of adult education. I cannot argue with this objection. Worldview construction is, *de facto,* a surpassingly inclusive process. If relationships can be found between worldview construction and many of the ideals enunciated by adult education theorists, it is because worldview construction is a complex concept that serves as a focus of confluence for these ideals. Worldview construction is such a fundamental human activity—such a primary concern of *Dasein*—that most goals stated as proper to adult education will find correspondence with the concept of worldview construction.

WORLDVIEW CONSTRUCTION: TWO IDEOLOGIES

There are many ways of thinking of adult education, many schools of thought vis-a-vis the practice of adult education, many philosophies of adult education. Various schools of thought were categorized by John Elias and Sharan Merriam in their influential work on the philosophical foundations of adult education. Liberal Adult Education has its origins in classical Greek philosophers; emphasis is placed on the development of intellectual powers and the mastery of specific knowledge. Progressive Adult Education originated in the progressive movement in politics and concerns for social progress. The progressive movement envisioned social change as taking place through the instrumentality of education. Behaviorist Adult Education is rooted in modern philosophical and scientific movements, and fosters behavior modification and learning through reinforcement. Humanistic Adult Education is related to existentialism and humanistic psychology; key concepts are freedom and autonomy. Radical Adult Education springs from the same soil that nurtured Marxism, socialism and left-wing Freudianism. Finally, Analytic Adult Education originated in logical positivism and British analytic philosophy.[8]

Which of these philosophies can function most effectively as a basis for the facilitation of worldview construction? The Elias-Merriam classification scheme is helpful for sorting out the tendencies of various theorists and arranging these tendencies in some kind of order. I wish to employ a different arrangement, however, for understanding adult education philosophies. I prefer to view competing schools of thought in terms of points on a continuum. The extreme ends of the continuum are represented by two theoretical positions regarding adult education practice: the ideology of the Right and the ideology of the Left.

What distinguishes these ideologies fundamentally is their orientation toward time. Ideologues of the far Right fix their gaze lovingly on the past. Nostalgia is a foremost governing emotion. The past represents, and must always represent, the standard for thinking, willing, and doing; the past sets out ideals and values that must never be violated. Looking to the past the ideologue of the far Right sees a pristine Garden of Eden that is forever normative for human affairs.

On the other hand, the ideologue of the far Left despises the past and has fallen in love with an idealized and often romanticized future, a utopia. Utopia is normative for present action: Whatever is in tune with the desired future is correct and even required. Hope in the future is the inspiring virtue: the Garden of Eden is located in the future. The past is no more; the heritage of the past must be criticized and, finally, destroyed for the sake of the future.

The question, then, is this: What kind of educational intervention or program, as an expression of an underlying ideology, is most promising for the facilitation of worldview construction among adults? The question cannot be avoided. Educational programs are designed and implemented by human beings. Human beings have prejudices, assumptions, and beliefs that eventually find instantiation in what they do. Everyone has an ideology, even the person who claims freedom from ideology. Not to choose is to choose; not to have an ideology is to have an ideology that maintains it is possible to be perfectly "objective" in viewing the world. Where should the adult educator strive to take a position on the continuum of philosophies?

The Ideology of the Right

By ideology I mean quite plainly a distinctive manner of thinking characteristic of a group of persons. Let it be given that the various points on the continuum of philosophical thinking about adult education represent definite theoretical positions if not full-blown theories. Both ends of the continuum are extreme. Any description of either end of the continuum will approach caricature. Caricature, however, is sometimes helpful for delineating the salient features of any speculative position.

Thinkers located on the far Right, if not completely antiquarian, are enamored of the past. They prize tradition (defined in a narrow sense), continuity, and authority. Through the instrumentality of adult

education, it is thought, learners are furnished with obediential poten-
cies, habits of mind, and particular ways of addressing controversial
issues. If there is to be change, change must come through evolutionary
processes and not through revolution. The principal attribute of correct
evolutionary processes is gradualism, a gradualism that is fearful and cau-
tious of any kind of change. The primacy of order is assumed. There can
be no authentic advance unless it is orderly. Ideally education forms
adults for useful lives within an established order in which social, economic, political, and ethical norms are prescribed. The adult educator is
the authority figure who decides what must be learned. Paternalism is
the central feature of far Right thinking about adult education.

Ideologies of the Right are not currently in vogue. Liberal Adult Education is the school of thought most likely to tilt toward the Right end of
the continuum. Liberal Adult Education, in the classical sense of liberal
which indicates the kind of education identified as appropriate for the
leisure classes, has relatively few supporters today. Egalitarian dogmas
have leveled differences between intellectual elites and academic under-
achievers, between the well-educated and the hardly educated. Nonetheless educational programs for adults that tend toward the Right of the
continuum still exist today.

The Right: A Scenario

Assume an adult educator responsible for library-based adult education programs wishes to conduct a discussion program that deals directly
with worldview construction. The educator is concerned that most
adults today lack familiarity with the great classical texts of antiquity. A
discussion program is developed employing an approach similar to the
Great Books model. The program is organized on several assumptions.
First, adults need to read some of the classics of Western civilization.
Whether they recognize this need is not really relevant; the need for cultural literacy is never recognized by the masses. Second, adults need a
leader who selects the classics that will be read and discussed. Unaware
of their need for cultural literacy the prospective participants in the program will also be unable to choose the correct books. Third, adults need
someone to sequence, direct, and monitor learning activities. The adult
educator serves a police function while professing to be the keeper of
the truth.

The adult educator, in this scenario, is an authority or expert. Adults
are dependent, ill-informed, and unable to determine what is necessary
for them to discuss their worldviews intelligently. Further, they are
incapable of taking control over the content of the discussions. What is

central to the program, of course, is the agenda of the adult educator and not the concerns of the participants relating to worldview construction. The adult educator, in effect, wishes to promote his or her own worldview as normative.

The Ideology of the Left

Thinkers on the Left of the continuum are utopian; they are principally interested in using education as a tool of social engineering for the creation of utopian societies that are described almost exclusively in political and economic terms. They reject traditional ways of thinking and take pride in being members of the *avant garde.* Education is to be used to liberate adults from false consciousness. Learners must critique their assumptions about themselves and others. Evidence that such criticism is effective is adduced when learners experience a transformation of their perspectives and confess their former sins of wrong thinking. Education is primarily emancipatory. The adult educator is a change agent. If the adult educator of the far Right is paternalistic, the adult educator of the far Left is messianic.

Ideologies of the Left are predominant in the literature of adult education today. Neo-Marxist doctrines, particularly the doctrine that views the process of history as determined by class struggle and oppression, are favored in not a few academic centers by professors and the perfervid graduate students who come under their influence. The element of Progressive Adult Education that stresses social change together with Radical Adult Education constitute a major force in the theoretical foundations of adult education today, on many campuses if not elsewhere. One is hardly a member of the club in good standing, in many circles, if he or she does not frequently talk about liberation and emancipation with great earnestness.

A Scenario: The Left

Suppose an adult educator desires to arrange a discussion program that addresses worldview construction. An approach not unlike Jack Mezirow's perspective transformation model is used.[9] The adult learners are assumed, to some degree, to be victims of oppression. Whatever evil happens in their lives, it is further assumed, is attributable solely to the machinations of oppressors, the perversity of society, or unfair economic conditions. Oppressors cannot be trusted to be other than oppressors;

they can never change oppressive patterns. The dialectical struggle between bourgeois oppressors and exploited masses is inevitable and ongoing.

The adult educator takes the role of emancipator. Under the guidance of the adult educator learners will put aside their false consciousness or distorted ways of thinking and experiencing the world. The adult educator, of course, defines the nature of false consciousness and determines when the learner's critique of false consciousness has been adequate, i.e., when a change of heart or conversion has taken place. The political agenda of the adult educator controls the discussion process. The adult educator serves a police function while professing to be a liberator. In effect the adult educator holds forth his or her worldview as normative.

A CRITIQUE OF THE RIGHT AND LEFT

It is a peculiar truth that as extremes of the continuum are approached, both Right and Left thinking becomes similar in many aspects. The ideologue of the Right wishes to assure the correct thinking that has been sanctioned by tradition and so exerts control over the structure and topics of discussion by prescribing canonical texts. The ideologue of the Left desires to eradicate the false thinking inherited from the past, thereby assuring movement toward the blessed Utopia, and so exerts control by pronouncing learners victims and by defining the contents of authentic consciousness. The ideologues of both the Right and the Left claim to serve adult learners by empowering them: with time-tested knowledge (in the case of the Right) or with insight into their oppression (in the case of the Left).

This is not to argue that programs such as the Great Books program are *per se* nefarious or otherwise inappropriate as frameworks for discussion and learning. Nor is it to argue that programs such as Mezirow's perspective transformation are useless. Familiarity with important texts, even when they are prescribed and selected by the adult educator, can further the growth of adult learners since the reactions of adult participants to these texts cannot be easily controlled in any event. Participation in a program that helps learners identify and examine their hidden assumptions can result in greater self-understanding among the learners, and can provoke positive changes in the learner's behavior. It is a fact that too many adults are unfamiliar with classic texts; it is also a fact that many adults are, and have been, victims of oppression.

Ideologies of both the Right and the Left thrive because each of these ideologies have taken hold of a truth. But the truth that we must pay honor to the past has been so heavily emphasized by the extreme Right that it suffers distortion; the truth that we must seek justice for the oppressed, and help them attain justice, has been so fanatically argued by the extreme Left that it has become misshapen. What remains attractive about far Right and far Left ideologies is that they yet retain the sparkling glimmer of truths that have been abused by excessive enthusiasm.

What is argued here, and with insistence, is that the direct facilitation of worldview construction should be balanced ideologically and should make no suppositions about any adult learners who are able to function normally in a learning situation. We must be wary, I strongly urge, of adult educators who attempt to change the worldviews of adults by reliance on subtle mechanisms inspired by the educator's commitment to a particular ideology. Adult educators, in this regard, must be facilitators and not preachers, politicians, salespersons or others who fulfill legitimate roles in contexts other than the setting of education. Adult educators, in respect to worldview construction programs, must refrain from dominating the educational process or insinuating their personal views into that process. If educators want to influence social policy or exercise political influence in specific matters that are publicly disputed they should run for public office.

Impartiality

Is it possible for any adult education program directly concerned with worldview construction to be open in respect to its structure and unbiased as to the management of discussion content? The format for this kind of program exists under the name of Participation Training. This system for adult learning was explained in some detail in a previous chapter.

Is it possible for any adult educator to be an impartial facilitator of adult discussion and dialogue? I respond to this question with an unequivocal "yes." If the word professional means anything at all in relation to the practice of adult education it should imply that facilitators of adult learning are able to restrain their speech acts, moderate their enthusiasms, and refrain from exerting influence on learners to accomplish personal agendas.

Not only is such impartiality possible but it seems that ethical considerations require moderation. To use the office of teacher and all of the legitimacy that surrounds the office to attempt to change a person's worldview is a betrayal of the office. Thomas Singarella and Thomas Sork raise the ethical question of whether adult educators should aspire to change social systems through their influence on changing individuals. "If the goal of the transaction is to produce individual change, then the adult educator is accountable to the individual learner. But if the goal is change in social systems, then to whom is the adult educator account-able?"[10] Clearly the adult educator as citizen is entitled to the full exer-cise of free speech. The adult educator as teacher or professor should be unhampered in expressing even the most unenlightened opinion in the ordinary classroom setting. But when it comes to efforts, whether overt or subtle, to adjust the adult learner's values, beliefs, feelings, and life practices in a context specifically designed for the sharing and evaluation of learner worldviews, the responsibility of the adult educator to be impartial outweighs his or her right to engage in persuasive behaviors. Granted, adults are ordinarily not as susceptible as children to the influ-ence of authority figures. Nonetheless adults have the right to a context as free of educator influence as possible when they come together to share and examine their existing worldviews. We would be repelled by the idea of a Presbyterian adult educator who tries to influence, either openly or covertly, the members of a discussion group in a Jewish retire-ment home to convert to the Presbyterian church. We should also be concerned when an adult educator attempts to insinuate his or her polit-ical beliefs into the thinking of adult learners.

Not all adult educators, it seems, agree with the above judgment. Phyl-lis Cunningham states that adult educators who claim to be apolitical are making a political statement because what one says while declaring neu-trality (her word) is "that one is quite satisfied with the present organiza-tion of social relationships and the distribution of resources in society." It can be argued, Cunningham declares, that adult educators invent such ideas as scientific objectivity "to sanitize our basic desires to maintain inequality, racism, sexism, and classicism since we are satisfied, on bal-ance, with our 'share of the pie.'"[11]

If Cunningham is suggesting that adult educators must oppose in prin-ciple any form of injustice or discrimination based on racial, gender, or class biases, I have no argument with her. It is not my position that the adult educator should be impartial when it comes to general ethi-cal norms and the general principles that govern a society espousing equality of opportunity. Every adult educator should teach, by exam-ple if not byword, that every person deserves just treatment, that civility is better than boorishness, and that moderation is a virtue. Unfor-tunately, some teachers, in the course of their teaching, have been known to endorse particular political parties and political candi-dates. The accusation of racism, sexism, and classicism to impugn the motives of those who may honestly disagree with a theoretical position is not unheard of in the field of adult education. At times it seems as if the terms racism, sexism, and classicism have become code words used to suppress dissent.

Self-appointed defenders of ideological purity occasionally become extremely prescriptive in support of their views. A case in point: the oral presentation guidelines for the Midwest Research-to-Practice Conference in Adult, Continuing and Community Education caution that careful attention must be taken to avoid the use of sexist language or language which *could be* (emphasis mine) construed as ethnically biased. Just about any language could be construed as ethnically biased by anyone wishing to attack the motives of a speaker. Language police are to be feared because thought police usually follow in their wake.

To practice impartiality as a facilitator of an educative process could mean, as Cunningham notes, that one is content with the *status quo,* but it does not necessarily mean this. Perhaps no one can remain neutral, but the question is one of impartiality and not neutrality. Impartiality can also mean that an adult educator, despite strong feelings and a definite position on sociopolitical issues, does not wish to co-opt any learner's right to define problems anent social relationships and resource distribution in our society. To opt for impartiality may mean that the adult educator judges it is ethically wrong to perpetrate an invasion of another's mind. In other words, the adult educator does not wish to adopt a messianic or paternalistic posture; the impartial adult educator does not equate critical thinking with his or her thinking.

TRUTH AND CONVERSATION

Responding to the perennial question "What is truth?" philosophers have formulated various theories. The correspondence theory of truth is perhaps the most well known. Truth is defined, according to Aristotle and Thomas Aquinas, as the "adequation of things and the intellect." Elizabeth Steiner notes that this is best interpreted by saying truth is "the correspondence of our beliefs to reality."[12] At present these words are being typed on a computer screen. If somehow I believed I was using a quill pen, there would be no commensuration between what is in my mind and the actual state of affairs. When my mind reflects the actual state of affairs, the theory proposes, I possess the truth.

Intuitively the correspondence theory makes sense. Some critics, however, question whether there can be a correspondence between mind and objects. They prefer to think of truth in terms of the coherence of ideas. A statement or idea is true only if it is consistent with other statements or ideas that have been accepted as true. What constitutes truth is the coherence that exists among all the ideas one possesses. While the correspondence theory of truth views truth in the light of relationships between the knower and that which is known, the coherence theory views truth in the light of relationships among all logical truths that have been known and are being known by the knowing subject.

The pragmatic theory of truth maintains that a statement, idea or proposition is true if it leads to practical consequences, if it works. If any notion is productive of positive outcomes, according to the pragmatic theory of truth, it can be called true. A belief or thought is true if it has results such as ". . . control, predictive value, or if it stimulates creative inquiry, resolves problems in science and everyday life, makes us happy."[13]

Each of these theories of truth, while emphasizing important aspects of truth, has its weaknesses. The strongest theory is, by default, the correspondence theory. Pragmatism affords many insights but fails to provide a ground for investigations of ultimate questions. A description of the world in regard to its ultimate meaning may make me happy or encourage additional inquiry. If such a description, however, does not approximate a disclosure of "how it actually is" with the world, the description is meaningless. With the coherence theory of truth one never seems to get outside one's own ideas. An illusion can be internally consistent with other illusions without having any reference to the world that exists independently of mind. But there are problems even with the correspondence theory.

If there is a world "out there" separate from myself, who is "in here," the task becomes one of finding a method that will faithfully bring to mind what is "out there." But we know that in any act of apprehending the world "out there" our assumptions, beliefs, biases, and so forth are projected from "in here" to the external world. There is no perfect objective knowledge; what we know of the world that exists independently of mind is awash in subjectivity since the act of knowing is a subjective act. Not only is an exact method required, therefore, but also a scrupulously correct analysis of human understanding.

After three centuries of searching since the time of Descartes, philosophers have neither achieved an undisputed understanding of human understanding nor have they designed a method that produces purely objective knowledge. Epistemology, the branch of philosophy that investigates the nature and limits of human knowledge, has been wounded and has fled the field of combat relinquishing property rights to pyschology. Psychology, in turn, has spawned dozens of theories or mental constructs spun out of the private assumptions of individual psychologists with the result that psychology is not so much an organized field of study as it is, in the main, a country fair of fragmentary competing hypotheses.

"The confusion and barrenness of psychology," wrote Wittgenstein, "is not to be explained by calling it a 'young science'; its state is not comparable with that of physics, for instance, in its beginnings . . . For in psychology there are experimental methods and conceptual confusion. (As in the other case conceptual confusion and methods of proof.) We think we have the method for solving problems but method and problems", according to Wittgenstein, "pass one another by."[14]

Neither epistemology nor psychology can establish exact definitions of the nature or limits of knowledge. Nor have philosophers determined what methods will bring us certainty and so-called objective truth. The burden of Gadamer's major opus *Truth and Method* was to show that methodology in itself cannot lead to the discovery of truth. No matter what method we use to examine the world, human beings are constrained to examine the world only as "insiders," only as "parts" of the whole. We cannot extricate ourselves from the world to gain the kind of perspective that would assure our ability to grasp even feebly the objective and certain truth of the world. In last analysis whatever we hold about the world (in relation to questions of ultimate, penultimate, or personal concerns) is held by belief. The content of our beliefs is important but equally important are the grounds for beliefs. These grounds are evaluated when we uncover the world through conversation.

Unveiling the World: Conversations

For Martin Heidegger truth is *aletheia*. This means more than simply identifying the Greek word for truth. *Aletheia* may be translated into English as truth, but etymologically it means unconcealment. To attempt to discover the truth of anything means to strip away whatever distorts the view of the thing, to unveil the thing. The unveiling of anything allows it to "appear" in the dynamism of its being. The Greek notion of *physis*, states Heidegger, is directly related to the meaning of *aletheia*. *Physis* denotes self-blossoming emergence, ". . . opening up, unfolding, that which manifests itself in such unfolding and perseveres and endures in it: in short, the realm of things that emerge and linger on."[15] Thus, the nature of a thing is revealed as its reality extrudes into the world of beings, as it ex-ists or thrusts itself forward ontically, i.e., as it is manifest in its existence.

Aletheia refers to the action of those who recognize the emergence of things. Something appears in the order of reality independent of mind but is revealed, is known, in the order of reality that comprises mind. For something to be unveiled, it must be thrusting forward ontically; it must also be a target of a consciousness that struggles against confusion or distortion. Something becomes true, becomes unveiled, when it is in the process of being known actively by someone.

Heidegger notes that in proposing his definition of truth, "we have not shaken off the tradition, but we have appropriated it primordially."[16] What he means here is that he has not rejected the correspondence theory of truth but has interpreted the notion of truth—*aletheia*—in the connotation used by the early Greek philosophers. It is not a matter of the mind simply registering an object of knowledge or coming into line so that it corresponds to the objective world. Instead, the mind, so to speak, actively unveils that-which-is-known as that-which-is-known simultaneously manifests itself in its ontic blossoming-out.

Two erroneous paths of thinking are blocked by reason of Heidegger's definition. First, the thinking that makes the mind the passive receiver of the objective world is rejected. Not to reject this way of thinking is to agree, at least implicitly, that human beings are dominated by their environments. Human beings, in other words, are viewed as merely reactive to environmental stimuli. Second, the thinking that makes the mind the creator of the objective world is rejected. I know more than my ideas of the world; I know the world ontically. Not to reject the radical idealism that questions the existence of the world independent from mind is to espouse solipsism which makes philosophy and dialogue with others impossible.

My interpretation of Heidegger's thought is necessarily brief but shows that truth must be understood as an unveiling in two ways: in respect to the emerging of the thing itself and in respect to its detection by an observer. Whatever is known, other than ideas, is known because of its own reality and because it is apprehended by a knower.

Apply these notions to worldview construction. The world exists. That is, it is present to consciousness as something that is blossoming forth. It has a history but nevertheless endures. It is potentially knowable from an almost infinite number of vantage points or perspectives in space and in time. Each individual possesses the ability to know the world and yet each person is "contained" in the world; each person is able, however, to unveil the world progressively until he or she attains an interpretive understanding from an almost infinitely small peephole on reality. Each person's view of the world is relative to a particular time, place, culture, language, and so forth. Absolute truth exists but it is available only in a God's-eye view of the world, a view that is not given to us. We comprehend absolute truth in a relative manner. And at no time in our lives can we say that the truth of the world is fully unconcealed. Our truths are partial, distorted, narrow. We see in a glass darkly.

None of us can lay claim to absolute truth, to certainty, to a purely "objective" understanding untainted by our biases. All we can claim is that each of us is possessor of an interpretation of the world, an interpretation based on limited experience. If we would aspire to a fuller understanding of the world, it must come only in conversation with others. The American philosopher Richard Rorty writes: "Hermeneutics sees the relations between various discourses as those of strands in a possible conversation, a conversation which presupposes no disciplinary matrix which unites the speakers, but where the hope of agreement is never lost so long as the conversation lasts. This hope is not a hope for the discovery of antecedently existing common ground, but simply hope for agreement, or, at least, exciting and fruitful disagreement."[17] Rorty's remarks addressed the community of philosophers directly but also apply, I suggest, to any individuals involved in the process of worldview construction. Each person who discusses his or her worldview with others, or enacts this worldview publicly, takes part in an ongoing conversation.

In union with others, in a community of interpreters, we can peel back the veils that obscure the world from inspection until we secure a more or less satisfactory explanation of the world in its ultimate, penultimate, and personal dimensions. When united in a conversation in which understandings and worldviews are shared, we stand a better chance of reducing the limitations and narrowness of our existing worldviews. This is a practical reason for engaging in conversations about our worldviews. There is another reason. Namely, there is, ineluctably, a social character to human understanding.

Conversation: Understanding as Social

The philosopher George Herbert Mead saw the knower and known "as two poles of a common experiential continuum woven within and by a common fabric of social intercourse." Mead was able to avoid talking about "objective" truth but he did not view knowledge as something produced by society alone; knowledge also is a function of objective inquiry. Mead "posited a 'field theory' of human experience within which the world, both physical and social, and the self are poles of dimensions."[18] Meaning comes into existence as shared meaning, and within a field of human relationships. My worldview can exist only in a world where there are many worldviews.

As a child I was exposed to the worldviews of my parents and relatives as these worldviews were enfolded in the tradition I received. With this tradition-cum-worldview I experienced the world and interpreted it in a definite way. I did not create my private meanings out of whole cloth;

meanings were available to me only within a community, some of which I took and made my own. As an adult I came into contact with the world-views of others and was thus able to bring further definition and renewal to my worldview. Because of exposure to other worldviews, worldviews that are even alien or contradictory, my worldview has undergone changes. I am better able to lift veils from aspects of the world of which I was never aware. In conversation with others, and conversation here is broadly construed, diverse meanings are available to me. In conversation with others I am able to find new understandings and assimilate these understandings into my own worldview. In conversation with others I am able to correct elements of my worldview that are lacking.

There is perhaps no better way of realizing the social matrix in which worldviews gestate and are born than by reference to language. How we understand the world is conditioned largely by the language available to us when tradition is transmitted or when we express ourselves about any issue. Now language is a social invention. At least two people are required before any true language can come into existence. Since there is also a close connection between thought and language, it can be said that thinking itself, in some substantive way, is dependent on language. And if thinking is contingent upon language, so also are different forms of knowing and, finally, so also is understanding itself.

Conversation: Unveiling Understanding and Self

The attempt to unveil the truth of the world through conversation is, at another level of thought, an attempt to unveil one's worldview or interpretive understanding of the world. This is so because we speak about the world in reference to our own frameworks of understanding. In conversation we unveil our ideas, values, beliefs, and positions we have taken vis-a-vis the world. Perhaps for the first time we come to understand our understandings of the world because we have expressed these understandings in a public forum. On occasion I have voiced an opinion that I had not articulated previously and have, for the first time, "heard" the opinion; frequently this "hearing" of my own opinion in a group context has made me aware of the shortcomings of the opinion. What remains unexpressed is often inchoate, indistinct, and even mud-dled. Ideas are sometimes refined only when they are written or when they are manifested in speech acts.

Earlier it was mentioned that given the human condition we are not privy to absolute knowledge but must rely, in final analysis, on beliefs. Even my awareness of the chair in which I am sitting is dependent on my belief that my neurological functioning is normal. When we participate in conversations with others we expose a wide range of beliefs for assessment and evaluation. We also offer reasons or grounds for our beliefs. Sometimes our beliefs are challenged. Sometimes the grounds for particular beliefs are found by others to be shaky. We may change some beliefs thereby changing, to some extent, our worldviews. What takes place when beliefs and reasons for beliefs are examined during a conversation is the unveiling of aspects of worldview. What has been hidden or covered is made manifest. The truth comes out. Interpretive understanding is itself understood in a new way.

All of this, of course, entails the unveiling of self. When one expresses a worldview or an aspect of one's understanding of the world in the company of others, and when others offer different views, an unveiling of self occurs. There is no need to resort to various psychotherapeutic paradigms to facilitate self-understanding. The truth of one's self is uncovered in the unveiling of one's worldview. Every person, after all, has been shaped by his or her tradition, by experience; every person's worldview is related intimately to his or her identity. One's worldview coincides, in important ways, with one's being-in-the-world. How I comport myself in the world, how I enact my being, is directly related to my interpretive understanding of the world. The discovery of what I really believe about the world in response to the questions that arise out of ultimate, penultimate, and personal concerns is virtually equivalent to self discovery.

The question that remains is this: Is there any way of organizing a conversation wherein adults may examine one another's, and their own, worldviews? In other words, what kind of educational activity can be structured to help adults unveil the truth of the world (insofar as this truth is accessible), the truth of their worldviews, and the truth of their being-in-the-world? The question has already been answered to some extent in the previous chapter on the structuring of conversation. Participation Training is at least one approach among many that promises to bring adults together for effective group discussion.

SUMMARY

A number of theorists have argued that adult education has goals transcendent to the learning of the content immediately at hand. It is suggested that worldview construction is a goal that encompasses the transcendent goals identified by others.

Two competing ideologies, each representing an extreme end of the continuum of adult education philosophies, are to be avoided to permit adult learners to construct their own worldviews without the interference of the facilitator of worldview construction. Facilitators of worldview construction must strive to remain impartial even if neutrality in matters of social concern is impossible.

Heidegger's interpretation of the meaning of truth as a process of unveiling is emphasized. The truth process is best undertaken by a community of interpreters who share their experiences and understandings with one another.

REFERENCES

1. For an excellent review of the connection between the philosophy of N. F. S. Grundtvig and the ideas of Eduard Lindeman, see Clay Warren's "Andragogy and N. F. D. Grundtvig: A Critical Link" in *The Adult Education Quarterly,* Vol. 39, No. 4, 1989, pp. 211–23.

2. The best source for information about Grundvig's philosophy is Hal Koch's *Grundtvig.* Translated by Lewellyn Jones, the book was published in New York by the Antioch Press in 1952.

3. Lindeman, Eduard. *The Meaning of Adult Education.* Montreal: Harvest House, 1961, p. 5. For a brief yet thorough analysis of Lindeman's influence on the development of American adult education see Stephen Brookfield's "The Contribution of Eduard Lindeman to the Development of Theory and Philosophy in Adult Education," *Adult Education Quarterly,* Vol. 34, No. 4, 1984, pp. 185–96.

4. Bergevin, Paul. *A Philosophy for Adult Education.* New York: The Seabury Press, 1967, pp. 31–40. Bergevin's reliance on Aristotle is not completely clear from the text of *A Philosophy for Adult Education.* Bergevin's classroom lectures, however, dwelled extensively on the value of Aristotle's ideas, particularly the notion of the golden mean and the avoidance of extreme positions on various continua of opinion. "Steer to the middle path," Bergevin encouraged.

5. This is a close paraphrase. I did not write out Bergevin's exact words.

6. Apps, Jerold. *Toward A Working Philosophy of Adult Education.* Syracuse: Syracuse University Publications in continuing Education, 1973, pp. 58–59.

7. Brookfield, Stephen. "A Critical Definition of Adult Education," *Adult Education Quarterly.* Vol. 36, No. 1, 1985, p. 46. Brookfield believes that "received assumptions" can be jettisoned thereby signifying the adult has become autonomous. Also, he seems to believe that everything received from one's past has been received uncritically. I agree with his emphasis on the need for ongoing assessment of assumptions but argue that we never completely transcend the traditions we have received nor must we in order to be critical thinkers.

8. Elias, John & Merriam, Sharan. *Philosophical Foundations of Adult Education.* New York: Krieger Publishing Company, 1980, pp. 9–11.

9. Mezirow defines perspective transformation as "the emancipatory process of becoming critically aware of how and why the structure of psycho-cultural assumptions has come to constrain the way we see ourselves and our relationships, reconstituting this structure to permit a more inclusive and discriminating integration of experience and acting upon these new understandings." Cf. Mezirow's "A Critical Theory of Adult Learning and Education," *Adult Education,* Vol. 32, No. 1, p. 6. I cite Mezirow's work as exemplifying the Left not because of the radicalness of his thinking but because his work represents the most thoughtful expression of a Left-leaning theory in the United States, and a theoretical position with which many adult educators are familiar. Also, it seems to me, perspective transformation is obviously open to abuse at the hands of self-styled saviors of the adult masses and for this reason lends easily to the exemplification of far Left ideology. For an analysis of Mezirow's thinking see the article by Susan Collard and Michael Law "The Limits of Perspective Transformation: A Critique of Mezirow's Theory," *Adult Education Quarterly,* Vol. 39, No. 2, 1989, pp. 99–107. See also Jack Mezirow's reply in "Transformation Theory and Social Action: A Response to Collard and Law," in *Adult Education Quarterly,* Vol. 39, No. 3, 1989, pp. 169–75.

10. Singarella, Thomas & Sork, Thomas. "Questions of Values and Conduct: Ethical Issues for Adult Education." *Adult Education Quarterly,* Vol. 33, No. 4, 1983, p. 249.

11. Cunningham, Phyllis. "The Adult Educator and Social Responsibility," in Ralph Brockett (ed.) *Ethical Issues in Adult Education.* New York: Teachers College, Columbia University, 1988, p. 136.

12. Steiner, Elizabeth. *Methodology of Theory Building.* Sydney, Australia: Educology Research Associates, 1988, p. 59. Heidegger delineated the lineage of the correspondence theory of truth by tracing it from Aristotle to Isaac Israeli to Avicenna to Thomas Aquinas. Cf. Heidegger's *Being and Time.* Translated by John Macquarrie and Edward Robinson. New York: Harper and Row, 1962, p. 257.

13. Angeles, Peter. *Dictionary of Philosophy.* New York: Barnes and Noble, 1981, p. 298.

14. Wittgenstein, Ludwig. *Philosophical Investigations.* Translated by G. E. M. Anscombe. New York: Macmillan, 1st Printing, 1968, p. 232e.

15. Heidegger, Martin. *An Introduction to Metaphysics.* Translated by Ralph Manheim. New York: Anchor Books, 1961, p. 11.

16. Heidegger, Martin, op. cit., *Being and Time,* p. 262.
17. Rorty, Richard. *Philosophy and the Mirror of Nature.* Princeton: Princeton University Press, 1979, p. 318.
18. Gill, Jerry. "Objectivity and Social Reality: Peter Berger's Dilemma," *Philosophy Today.* Vol. 32, No. 3, 1988, p. 265.

Chapter Eight

THE PURPOSES OF ADULT EDUCATION:
CONCLUDING THOUGHTS

A worldview is both a perspective in time and culture from which a person "sees" or experiences the world and a person's interpretive understanding of the world in terms of ultimate, penultimate, and immediate personal concerns. Tradition is a privileged kind of experience that derives from a particular frame of reference. This frame of reference, in turn, contains values, beliefs, assumptions, and patterns of thinking, feeling, and acting. While worldview construction occurs naturally, the process can be facilitated directly and explicitly when educators help adults structure discussions about worldview issues. Interventions on the part of educators can assist adults in meeting the obligation of worldview examination, an obligation that can be fulfilled by means of private reflection or group discussion. In facilitating worldview construction educators also aid adults in the development of their interpretive understandings of the world.

Over a decade ago I offered a definition of adult education that identified three ideal outcomes of the educational process for adults. Adult education, in a broad sense, ideally helps adults develop and actualize their various potentialities "to the end that the learners become more liberated as individuals, better capacitated to participate in the life of their communities and institutions, and empowered to create an authentically human future."[1] In this concluding chapter each of these themes is considered.

INDIVIDUAL LIBERATION

Liberation may be viewed and defined from various perspectives. Political liberation involves the freeing of persons from repressive political regimes and from legal systems that are appraised as unjustly discriminatory. Economic liberation is concerned with the freeing of people from poverty and from economic conditions that perpetuate poverty and its attendant miseries. Social liberation attempts to free people from social customs and norms that are unjustly restrictive. Religious liberation attempts to free people from a rudderless existence in which values are ignored and commitments are neglected. All forms of liberation seem to begin with a proper goal: the freeing of human beings from whatever curtails growth, restricts individual expression, or denies what persons are entitled to by virtue of membership in the human race.

Not all movements or schemes proclaimed as a liberating process, however, avoid excessive measures in moving toward the realization of goals. Nor do individuals, once liberated, maintain the delicate equilibrium that separates freedom from license. Once a "revolution" has been accomplished, it needs to be maintained. Little is accomplished if a repressive system is overthrown only to be replaced by a different repressive system. The moral high ground can be captured by those who play the role of liberator (often with an overabundance of self-righteousness) but this high ground can become a strategic point for the creation of different oppressive systems. Liberating movements can go sour. The oceans of misery created by Stalin and Hitler, representatives of the extreme Left and extreme Right respectively, under the banner of political and economic liberation should have instructed us that evil deeds are always camouflaged as noble endeavors by cynics adept in the techniques of manipulation.

In the 20/20 hindsight of history, of course, it is no great task to point out the depredations of a Hitler or Stalin. It is more risky to critique current trends and popular movements because: 1) there is relatively little evidence on which to base judgments of current trends and 2) it is difficult to counter ideas enshrined as dogmas by the supporters of popular movements. Nonetheless the time is long overdue to critique so-called radical adult education, the school of thought that views the adult educator as a political/economic/ideological liberator; the time has come to define liberation as something that occurs within the individual learner.

Some may argue that radical adult education is not a popular movement. In a sense this is correct. In the work-a-day world most adult educators are pragmatic and progressive, but radical adult education is assuredly the philosophy of choice in some major university adult education circles. The last haven for shop-worn ideologies is often a university campus.

The New Bankers

The neo-Marxist Christian theoretician Paulo Freire enjoyed a huge success with his denunciation of the "banking" system of education. Under the "banking" system the teacher makes deposits in the minds of the learners and checks these deposits occasionally by means of tests. Knowledge is conceived as a gift bestowed by the teacher (who knows everything) to the learners (who know nothing).[2] Freire's elucidation of the "banking" system of education as a means of oppression struck respondent chords in many adult educators who emphasized the participation of experienced adults in learning activities. Very few commentators recognized Freire had created a straw man for easy burning in his explication of the "banking" system. Not all adult educators, it is safe to say, bothered to read the philosophical justification Freire offered in support of his general contention the adult educator must contribute to social and political ferment, to keep the pot of unrest cooking, so to speak, by a constant stirring of resentment among the poor. At the heart of Freire's philosophy was the belief in the Marxist doctrine that class struggle is the iron law of history.[3]

What has happened in the two decades since *Pedagogy of the Oppressed* was first published in English is reminiscent of Orwell's *Animal Farm*[4] in that the "banking" method of education has been adopted by radical adult educators to accomplish their political agendas. Recently I discussed this phenomenon with someone involved in the liberation theology movement in Latin America. The educator was dismayed that "banking" education is now taking place within the liberation theology movement. At this historical juncture, it was observed, the privileged and unexamined content that is being banked in the minds of learners is neo-Marxist ideology, even when this ideology is falling into disrepute around the world.

Educators who fancy themselves political liberators are invading the minds of peasants telling them what values are necessary for their economic redemption. The "banking" system remains in place but the kind of currency is different. Those who are to be liberated from oppression no longer define their own reality; this is done for them by their liberators. The liberators define the nature of "false" consciousness and require that "true" consciousness (the consciousness of the liberator) be attained. The old imperialism is on the decline; the new imperialism is ready to take its place. The old dogma is dead; a new dogma lives.

Authentic liberation, the most profound kind of liberation, I propose, is not deliverance from economic injustice or political oppression, but instead liberation from interpretive understandings of the world that are permanently fixed, narrow, passive, uncritical, and other-disdaining, kinds of worldviews described in Chapter Four. This is not to say that economic, social, and political conditions are unimportant or irrelevant. Every adult educator as a citizen of a country wherein these conditions are oppressive has an obligation as a citizen to work for change; every adult educator as a member of the human race has an obligation to work for the amelioration of conditions that prevent adults from developing open, inclusive, active, discerning, critical, and other-accepting world-views. The adult educator *qua* educator, however, must refrain from invading the minds of adults and depositing therein any particular ideology. The adult educator, in the area of helping adults develop interpretive understandings, is first and foremost a facilitator.

It is not easy for an educator to maintain political impartiality in the teaching-learning situation, but impartiality can be practiced if the educator is capable of self-restraint and when an educational design such a Participation Training is used to structure discussions. Another factor supporting impartiality is the educator's respect for individual learners and confidence that they are supremely capable of interpreting their own experience and forming their own judgments. Adult educators find no difficulty in verbalizing their respect for the rights of others and the value of adults' experiences. Verbalization, however, is much easier than the translation of these words into practice.

The question that now comes to the fore is this: If the adult educator *qua* educator must remain politically impartial, on what grounds can the adult educator maintain that worldviews should ideally possess the characteristics of openness, inclusivity, autonomy, and positive regard for the worldviews of others? If the adult educator is not permitted to espouse political values, why should the adult educator be allowed to favor values relating to worldview construction? A satisfactory response to this question can be forthcoming only if a distinction is made between general principle and specific applications of principle.

Someone can agree in principle that human beings should not be economically oppressed. This is different, however, from the claim that a specific remedy—collectivism, capitalism, socialism—will surely relieve human beings of economic distress. People can agree on ends, goals, and principles and strongly disagree on means of accomplishing the ends, instruments for the attainment of goals, and particular actions that may bring principles to fruition. General principles can be established as valid on the basis of abstract reasoning. Disagreements ensue when individuals begin to discuss what is needed in the world of concrete realities to operationalize general principles. While most people will agree that a balanced national budget is a desideratum, some will argue that the solution lies in increased taxes, on the one hand, or cuts in spending, on the other hand.

The claim that worldviews should make possible an openness to new ideas and experiences, should avoid narrowness of vision, should influence the worldviewer to rely on his or her informed judgment, and should encourage the worldviewer to appreciate the worldviews of others is a claim that exists as a higher order principle. It is substantively different from the claim that a Methodist worldview is demonstrably better than a Presbyterian one.

Adults, then, can be helped to liberate themselves from whatever impedes the construction of open and inclusive worldviews, worldviews that not simply taken over with no reflection as convenient hand-me-downs. This kind of liberation is more lasting in the long term, more substantial, and more valuable than other kinds of liberation. Adults can be helped to liberate themselves for clear and creative thinking, for relating well with others, for valuing the feelings that contribute to the shaping of a human community, and for searching out ways of solving economic, social, and political problems.

PARTICIPATION

It has always been fashionable in certain circles to discern human nature as corrupt and brutal. Human beings are naturally aggressive. Their basic inclination is the inclination to violence. The history of the human presence on earth is written largely in terms of bloodshed, oppression, wars, and depredations of which lower animals are not capable. Examples of "man's inhumanity to man" abound and it is not surprising that some persons adopt a pessimistic view of human transactions. It is not even surprising that Marx would see class struggle and dialectical conflict as primary laws of human history. Under close analysis, however, the argument supporting the natural aggressiveness of human beings cannot stand.

Without denying evidences of human aggressiveness, acquisitiveness, and selfishness, it can be argued effectively that a high degree of collaboration, cooperation, and trust entered into the evolutionary scheme of things long ago and tilted the balance toward human survival. It is highly improbable that the human race would have survived unless cooperation, at some point in evolution, began to take precedence over conflict.

The complex technology employed in tribal hunting, for example, the planning and execution of stratagems of the hunt, required close collaboration and a planned division of labor. And when the hunt was successful, the fair distribution of food reinforced the willingness of individuals to work together in the future. Aggressiveness and brutality are well known in human history just as crimes are well known because of their prominence in the news media today. Not much was made historically about collaboration and trust because these characteristics were commonplace, expected, and steadily present in the affairs of human beings once a particular evolutionary threshold was crossed.

This fundamental relationship of partnership and emphasis on participatory effort is reflected in Heidegger's phenomenological analysis of the contemporary (relative to the long-time scale of human evolution) humanity. Being-with-others (*Mitsein*) is constitutive of being-human (*Dasein*). Heidegger seems to suggest that *Dasein* is on the way to authenticity when solicitude, considerateness, and forebearance characterize *Dasein*. That is, someone moves toward ontological authenticity when his or her mode of being-with-others is one of collaborativeness.[5]

I would add to this that the truth about oneself and the truth about others is uncovered maximally when self and others stand in an other-affirming relationship. To put this in simpler terms, without in the least becoming overly romantic, the truth of self is uncovered most profoundly, and the truth of another is revealed most profoundly, when self and other are committed to one another in a loving relationship. And by love I mean a disinterested or unselfish love, a love that holds the beloved in such esteem that no sacrifice is too great for the sake of the beloved.

On a more mundane plane, but no less important, human beings need to participate intelligently, compassionately, and actively in their institutions and communities to strengthen and increase the grip of altruism on the evolutionary process. Gordon Allport, interpreting the law of affective evolution formulated by the nineteenth century philosopher Auguste Comte, states this law holds "that with time there comes a diminution in the preponderance and intensity of personal inclinations, and a growth and extension of other-regarding sentiments."[6]

We never overcome self-love, nor should we, but self-love is not totally dominant. "In proportion as an individual is democratically socialized he finds it intolerable to seek happiness at the expense of others."[7] Perhaps the "law" of affective evolution is less a rigid law than a general strategy for the continuing evolution and survival of humanity. We move from egoism to altruism in order to accomplish dimly perceived goals of evolution, goals of universal peace and harmony that can be addressed most eloquently, at the present time, in terms of poetry and metaphor.

Paul Bergevin wrote of the need of adults to participate in the civilizing process. "The civilizing process is a corporate, social movement

involving the whole of society, as it moves from barbarism toward refine-
ment in behavior, tastes, and thought."[8] The civilizing process, Bergevin
averred, is an evolution through which individuals discover human capa-
bilities and implement human effort toward the realization of happiness.
Happiness is achieved, according to Bergevin, through the pursuit of
excellence, an ideal proposed originally by Aristotle.

The civilizing process does not proceed automatically any more than
evolution, at its present stage, proceeds without the choices and activities of human beings. Adults particularly must participate in the civilizing
process as individuals and, chiefly, as members of their institutions and
communities. This requires participation with others in service organizations, in local, regional, and national politics, in churches, and in community organizations that have a special appeal for each individual adult.
The participation, as noted above, must be intelligent, active, and com-
passionate in the sense that fellow-feeling, and not mere self-interest, is a
motivator of action.

To participate adequately in the civilizing process necessitates skill in
the identification of facts and issues; adequate participation requires the
ever-growing ability to think systematically, to bring intuitional insights
to bear on issues, and to enlighten understanding through hermeneutic
action. Social and political action needs to be informed; thoughtfulness
and understanding must be the ground for any kind of action that sets
about to improve the human condition. This is why the facilitation of
worldview construction should be a primary aim of every adult educator.

EMPOWERMENT

Sherman Stanage wrote that to empower a person "is to invest one formally or even legally with power or authority, or to authorize one as having certain power or powers. It is to impart or bestow power on persons
toward some end or for some specific purpose."[9] The description is
appropriate and straightforward. It is a description, however, that apparently enraged Jeff Zacharakis-Jutz judging from his fervent rhetoric.
Zacharakis-Jutz denounced the notion of empowerment as a charitable
process where power is given or bestowed on powerless people.
"Instead it is revolutionary, always antagonistic, and many times violent,
since one group is taking the power it was previously denied."[10]

Such bombast and fanaticism build upon the excesses of Freirean neo-
Marxism and fashions assumptions that are seldom challenged in university adult education circles. One of these assumptions is a vapid
egalitarianism that confuses equality before the law with equality of com-
petence and decries elitism of any kind. Particularly in university adult

education circles it is necessary to establish one's credentials as morally righteous. This is easily done by speaking out strenuously and frequently against elitism, often while maintaining a lifestyle that is nothing if not economically elitist.

A decade ago Isaac Asimov expressed dismay that attacks on elitism masked anti-intellectualism and supported a cult of ignorance. Anti-elitists were "nurtured by the false notion that democracy means that 'my ignorance is just as good as your knowledge.'"[11] Political ideologues of the Left, in their eagerness to identify with and redeem the oppressed masses, are seemingly unable psychologically to admit individual differences. Contrary to their dogmas, some people are better informed than others, some people are more competent than others, some people are more skilled than others, some people are more developed than others, and it is the obligation of those who are advantaged (materially, educationally, and socially) to help those who are disadvantaged.

This is not necessarily an obligation due out of charity, although this may be the case in some particular situations. Instead, this obligation is based on the realization that the human family cannot survive "half slave and half free." As a human family we share the same planet and a common future. If one does not help another out of a fellow-feeling, then at least one should help another out of enlightened self interest. What is not needed at this point of human history is an emphasis on the violent overthrow of oppressors. Violence begets violence. The rhetoric of resentment may sound good and cast the speaker in an herioc pose, but in the long term it leads largely to continued misery. In any event, while there are indisputably oppressors of the poor, many of the poor live in intolerable conditions not because of the intentionality of oppressors but because of the human inability to solve large-scale and almost intractable economic, social, and political problems. Not to understand this is to maintain a simplistic view of the real world.

Also, there is nothing wrong with charity rightly understood. If the bestowal of any good upon another person by a benefactor is accompanied, whether openly or tacitly, by the supposition that the benefactor has established dominance over the person receiving the good, this is not an act of charity. It is more properly understood as an act of domination. A charitable act is one motivated by a sense of fellow feeling that one has for another, by a sense of solidarity arising out of membership in the human family that unites rich and poor, educated and uneducated, powerful and weak. This sense of solidarity, in turn, is a by-product of a worldview that contains within itself the leaven of human authenticity.

Millions of adults need to be empowered. The corollary of this is that thousands of adult educators must assist adults in widening their perspectives, in acquiring new skills, and most important, in becoming more capable of interpreting the world. This does not make adult educators any better, any more noble, or any more deserving of praise than those who are helped. By virtue of membership in the human community all persons are of equal dignity.

There may be extreme situations wherein confrontation, and even violence, are necessary if groups of people are to experience empowerment. To make class struggle, resentment, and antagonism the standard operating procedure, the central principle motivating educational practice, however, bespeaks a dominant negativity and narrowness of vision that is morally reprehensible. The doctrine of class struggle surely has been a major force stimulating the emergence of twentieth century terrorism. A more authentic human future cannot be built on the basis of such a doctrine. If anything the doctrine of class struggle has the potential of poisoning and not redeeming the future.

CREATING A HUMAN FUTURE

Next to the discovery of the historicity of being or the blossoming awareness of cosmic evolution, the discovery of the possibility that human beings may have something to do with evolutionary outcomes ranks as momentous. Perhaps it is too much to ask individuals to believe their decisions have some bearing on future outcomes of cosmic evolution. It is within the bounds of reasonable imagination, however, to see the connectedness between individual human acts and future events within human history. I mentioned earlier that my existence was contingent upon existence of countless individual ancestors. If one of my great-great grandparents had not existed, I would not have come into being. The chance meeting of a young man and young woman at a party, my parents, resulted eventually in my birth, and now what I write in these pages, may have some impact on the thinking of others and how they go about making decisions.

There has been a network of persons and events that stretches from the deep past to the present moment; there is likewise a network of putative persons and events that will lead to some deep future outcome which will affect the lives of millions. To an extent yet unmeasured the future of a thousand years from now, if this future is to be realized, is in the hands of adults living today. What they think, what they know, and how they understand the world by virtue of their interpretations of the world can contribute to the creation of a world that matches the most noble human aspirations or the most dreadful human fears. Utopian dreams, impossible as they may presently seem, can be accomplished

given enough time and human care; the nightmare of political totalitari-
anism or, worse, global extinction, is also a possibility in the deep future.
It is necessary now that we at least entertain such thoughts seriously.
Teilhard de Chardin wrote that we need a "consciousness of being in
actual relationship with a spiritual and transcendent pole of universal
convergence."[12] He called this pole of convergence Point Omega. I
would settle for much less on the part of adults: a consciousness that
their decisions today, to a large extent, shape the landscape of the future.

Given this realization, this understanding, this sense of being posi-
tioned to construct a world, it follows that attentiveness to worldview
construction is necessary. This is due to the fact that adult decisions arise
out of their worldviews. Their decisions about how they comport themselves and how they live out their lives will be positively creative only to
the extent that positive creativity is permitted by their worldviews.

The precise nature of this deep ideal future cannot be described from
the present vantage point in human history. We rely on metaphor and
poetic imagery to describe that for which we strive. We long for a time
when swords will be turned into ploughshares, when the lion will lie
down with lamb, when universal peace and harmony characterize human
relationships. Some may question whether this vision of a more authentic
human future is simply a meaningless exercise of an overwrought imagination and whether the images of visionaries are too fanciful to have any
lasting impact on human understanding and behavior. I argue that without a vision of the future the human community has nothing for which to
spend its energies and that these unspent energies will be turned toward
destructive purposes. The largest drawback to progress are the deeds of
those who lack both imagination and vision.

Will not a focus on the building of a more authentic human future dis-
tract us from present problems and contemporary concerns? I think not.
We begin building the future by taking thoughtful action in the present.
The envisioning of a better future is what drives present creative activity.
For thousands of years it was supposed the Garden of Eden was in the
distant past. Perhaps it would be more correct to think of the Garden of
Eden as located in the indeterminate future. Its realization depends on
the actions, and worldviews, of those living today.

CONCLUSION

Matthias Finger's perceptive article on the new social movements and
their implications for adult education shows how adult education is
linked to the emerging crisis of modernity. The most salient truth proposed by modernity was that adults can be enlightened as a means of

achieving the goal of political emancipation. In the post-modern world "transformations are of an educational nature but not of a political nature; the relevant social and political transformations come 'from within' and happen at the level of the person."[13] This expresses most clearly a fundamental point of this book: The transformation of the world, politically, economically, and socially is not prior to the transformation of individuals but is a natural outcome of the orthogenetic development of individual worldviews, a "right" development that can be facilitated through educational processes.

SUMMARY

The facilitation of worldview construction is crucially important if the purposes of adult education are to be carried out successfully. Adults need to be liberated from anything that hampers their growth and creative activity; they need to be liberated for the tasks associated with the creation of more authentically future. All adults are called upon to participate in this work of making the future. They need to be empowered; those who are advantaged economically, socially, educationally, and politically must share their advantages in a spirit of solicitude knowing that in the sharing they are no better as human beings than those they help. In all of this adults require worldviews that are open, inclusive, active, critical, and other-accepting.

REFERENCES

1. McKenzie, Leon. *Adult Education and the Burden of the Future.* Washington, DC: University Press of America, 1978, p. iii.
2. Freire, Paulo. *Pedagogy of the Oppressed.* New York: Herder and Herder, 1971, pp. 57–74.
3. Marx, Karl & Engels, Friedrich. "The Communist Manifesto," in A. P. Mendel (ed.), *Essential Works of Marxism.* New York: Bantam Books, 1965, pp. 13–14.
4. Orwell, George. *Animal Farm.* New York: Signet, 1959.
5. Heidegger, Martin. *Being and Time.* Translated by John Macquarrie and Edward Robinson. New York: Harper and Row, 1962, p. 160.
6. Allport, Gordon. *Becoming.* New Haven: Yale University Press, 1955, p. 30.
7. Ibid., p. 30.
8. Bergevin, Paul. *A Philosophy for Adult Education.* New York: Seabury Press, 1967, p. 8.

9. Stanage, Sherman. "'Unrestraining' Liberty: Adult Education and the Empowerment of Persons," *Adult Education Quarterly,* Vol. 36, No. 2, 1986, p. 126.
10. Zacharakis-Jutz, Jeff. "Post-Freirean Adult Education: A Question of Empowerment and Power." *Adult Education Quarterly,* Vol. 39, No. 1, 1988, p. 45.
11. Asimov, Isaac. "A Cult of Ignorance," *Newsweek.* January 21, 1980, p. 19.
12. Teilhard de Chardin, Pierre. *The Phenomenon of Man.* New York: Harper Torchbook, 1959, p. 298.
13. Finger, Matthias. "New Social Movements and Their Implications for Adult Education," *Adult Education Quarterly,* Vol. 40, No. 1, 1989, p. 19.

Subject Index

Author Index